Here, There and Everywhere

Belonging, Identity and Equality in Schools

Derbyshire Advisory and Inspection Service

Edited and compiled by Robin Richardson

 DERBYSHIRE
County Council
Improving life for local people

Trentham Books
Stoke on Trent, UK and Sterling, USA

in   Department

Trentham Books Limited
Westview House   22883 Quicksilver Drive
734 London Road   Sterling
Oakhill   VA 20166-2012
Stoke on Trent   USA
Staffordshire
England ST4 5NP

© 2004 Derbyshire Advisory and Inspection Service (DAIS) and
Trentham Books

First published 2004, reprinted 2005

British Library Cataloguing-in-Publication Data
A catalogue record for this book is available from the British
Library

ISBN-13: 978-1-85856-343-5
ISBN-10: 1-85856-343-7

Designed and typeset by Trentham Print Design Ltd., Chester
and printed in Great Britain by Bemrose Shafron (Printers) Ltd,
Chester.

Contents

Please note:
each chapter apart from the first begins with its own table of contents

Views and voices

Throughout the book there are quotations to illustrate and enrich the main text.
They are listed below.

1. Wild with the joy of it, by Shyama Perera
2. Precious and beautiful, by Eric Newton
3. Resonate, by Rehana Ahmed
4. People again, by Anne Frank
5. Bound up in difference, by Rowan Williams
6. Who we are, by Tessa Jowell
7. A part to play, Home Office
8. Ask mummy, ask daddy, by John Agard
9. A foreign place, by Edward Said
10. Beyond their world, by Flora Thompson
11. The football match, anon
12. Insecurity, anger and hysteria, by Arun Kundnani
13. White men of European stock, by H.A.L.Fisher
14. Where was the balance? by Nitin Sahney
15. The same the world over, by Chris Patten
16. The smart without a name, by Charles Dickens
17. The worth of each individual, by Brian Wren
18. Seeing and approaching the other, Commission on Multi-Ethnic Britain
19. My badge of identity, by Shyama Perera
20. Within their hearts a dream, by Caryl Phillips
21. I often paint fakes, about Pablo Picasso
22. Belief in life, by Barbara Hepworth
23. Any multicultural society, about Sophia Shamin
24. Ordinary act, by Marina Warner
25. Starch in our backbones, by Maya Angelou
26. The nationality called runners, by Zafir Behlic
27. Ever more compelling, by John Eggleston
28. Damn fools, by Fiona MacCarthy
29. Never die, by Nelson Mandela
30. The desire to know, by Alice Walker
31. Groucho Club, by Maya Jaggi
32. How we survive, by Meera Syal
33. Did not even know, by Arnold Bennett
34. Exhilarating, by Rex Beddis
35. The landscape of our country, by Kazao Ishaguru
36. So they make sense, by Helen Dunmore
37. History so physically present, by Caryl Phillips
38. More and more powerful, by David Lodge
39. All for the price of a local call, by John O'Farrell
40. Why anyone needs to know, by John Cockcroft
41. Flourished all over the world, by Ray Hemmings
42. One equals one? by Munir Fasheh
43. Curse? by Anthony Burgess
44. Sweet melody, by Rabindranath Tagore
45. Unaware, by Andreas Fuglesang
46. Discovered and rediscovered, by Saadi Simawe
47. I want to be part, by Vikram Seth
48. Reverence, by Toru Takemitsu
49. Images from the imagination, by Michael Tippett
50. Open and free and curious, by Philip Pullman
51. We here, by Toni Morrison
52. All I needed to know, by Robert Fulgham
53. The ethics of the game, by C L R James
54. That noble game, by Abdulrazak Gurnah
55. You will always be Leeds, by Caryl Phillips
56. Quite slippery matter, by Shobana Jeyasingh
57. A kind of cleansing, by Rowan Williams
58. The little ones, by Sarah Maitland
59. This word spirituality, by David Hare
60. Let sleeping dogs lie? by Angela Wood
61. Centuries of trial and error, by Primo Levi
62. Use and conversion, by Iolo Wyn Evans
63. Eggshell delicacy, by Barbara Ward

1 INTRODUCTION
Here, There and Everywhere

The title

Students at a secondary school in a town in rural Derbyshire, working with students at a multi-ethnic school in Derby City some 20 miles away, set up a website. The purpose was to explore differences and similarities between the two schools and to share reports and reflections about various joint projects. Echoing a song performed by the Beatles, the students called the site *Here, There and Everywhere*. The same phrase is used now to summarise the spirit and concerns of this handbook. The handbook has been prepared for all Derbyshire schools – and for all other schools in Britain – and explores how issues of belonging, identity and equality are here, there and everywhere in every school.

The handbook draws on a range of projects organised by Derbyshire Advisory and Inspection Service in recent years. These include:

- a piece of forum theatre about prejudice and racism, *Sticks, Stones and Macpherson*, performed to audiences of teachers, administrative staff and school governors

- a set of guidance papers sent to all schools to support implementation of the letter and spirit of the Race Relations (Amendment) Act

- a working party of teachers and headteachers to advise on the expansion and refinement of the ideas in the guidance papers

- training events for all the staff in certain clusters of schools, with a focus on cross-phase discussion of each curriculum subject

- practical workshops for headteachers and for educational psychologists.

An account of the forum theatre presentation, and of the discussions it provoked in one cluster of schools, will valuably introduce the themes and concerns of this handbook as a whole.

Forum theatre

The concept of forum theatre was developed by the Brazilian theatre director Augusto Boal. He for his part was much influenced by the Brazilian educator Paulo Freire, whose best known book is *Pedagogy of the Oppressed*. In his approach to theatrical performance and to the role of theatre in relation to social justice, Boal was influenced by the German dramatist Bertolt Brecht.

A forum theatre presentation typically portrays a situation in which an individual or community is a victim of injustice. From time to time the action on stage is stopped and members of the audience are invited to make suggestions about how the unjust situation should be challenged. Typically they make the suggestions directly to the actors, with the actors for their part remaining in role. The actors then take on board the audience's suggestions and alter the story accordingly. Nevertheless, the presentation usually ends on a note of uncertainty and apparent defeat. It is up to the audience to think through the practical implications, not only for themselves as individuals but also for the community to which they belong.

Boal has said that the purpose of forum theatre, in the first instance, is to achieve a good debate rather than a good solution – a good debate being one in which people engage not only with their minds but also with empathy and emotional solidarity towards those who suffer from injustice, and with resolve to create better and fairer systems and relationships. The process of continually stopping the action and inviting the audience to interact with the characters means that the audience cannot sit back and be passive. Boal and Brecht saw a connection between passivity in front of a stage and passivity in the face of real events and situations. If audiences are prevented from being passive when they observe imaginary events, the theory claims, they are less likely to be passive in their dealings with reality.

When Derbyshire LEA planned its responses to the Stephen Lawrence Inquiry report it commissioned Actorshop, a forum theatre company based in London, to enact a story about racist incidents in schools and about how staff respond. The play was intended for audiences of teachers, administrative staff, mid-day supervisors and school governors and was in due course performed on several separate occasions in different parts of the county.

The story

The principal characters in *Sticks, Stones and Macpherson* are two Year 6 pupils, Patricia and Kerry. There are three other characters: Derek Brown and James Price, respectively the head and a class teacher at the school attended by Patricia and Kerry, and Patricia's mother Sue. Patricia's father is black and her mother is white. She is the only pupil in the school who is not white.

The first example of racism in the story arises shortly before an inter-school netball match. In the changing room a member of the opposing team says, when she sees Patricia, 'Oh, I thought we'd come to play netball, not to watch Planet of the Apes.' Patricia is distressed by the insult, particularly since it is greeted by sniggers from other members of her own team rather than by support for her. The insults and sniggers continue and in desperation she throws a ball hard into her tormentor's face and causes a copious nose bleed.

Patricia's teacher, James, sees the injured girl but knows nothing of why Patricia attacked her. He insists angrily that Pat should apologise and refuses to listen to anything she tries to say by way of explanation. He also brushes off Kerry, when she comes to her friend's defence. Patricia storms off home ('I'm sick of this stupid school') without taking part in the match.

Next day Patricia is in additional trouble because she went home without permission. James declares she must apologise in writing to the other school. She again refuses. There appears to be a total impasse but Kerry enters and manages to get James to listen to a full account of what actually happened. He realises that there was provocation and that he was too hasty in his judgement. Kerry also tells him that Pat and her mother frequently experience racism in the neighbourhood where they live. He agrees to go and visit them at their home.

When James visits them a few days later he is tongue-tied and awkward and gives no more than a garbled account of what happened. Sue jumps to the conclusion that Patricia has let her down by engaging in unprovoked violence and for a moment poor Patricia is utterly desolate and alone. But her mother

is loving and attentive and quickly listens and understands, and gives her daughter a powerful sense of moral support and solidarity.

James goes to see the headteacher, Derek Brown, to tell him about the racism that Sue and her mother frequently experience in the school's neighbourhood, and to tell him that Pat was provoked by racist insults. The head, however, is far more interested in a broken handbell that he is examining. ('I don't want to have to get a new bell, James, I really don't.') He acknowledges that he knows Patricia – 'that coloured kid' – but says the racism she has experienced isn't important, so far as he is concerned, since she will be transferring to a secondary school in a few months time. He reluctantly agrees, however, that James should organise an entertainment for parents on the theme of celebrating cultural diversity.

The head mutters also that James is welcome to convene a working party, if he would like to, to produce a school policy on race equality. 'I suppose it wouldn't be a bad idea to have a policy, come to think of it,' he adds. 'We're probably going to get other coloured kids in the future. The Home Secretary says schools like ours are in danger of being swamped by asylum-seekers and Muslims and people like that.'

The entertainment takes place a few weeks later and Pat is the star, appearing in it both as an African dancer and as an Indian dancer. James and the head congratulate her on a fine performance. Her mother approaches and the two teachers turn to her and remark that she must be very proud of her daughter. 'Yes,' says Sue, 'she's quite good for a nigger, isn't she? Though mind you, all niggers are pretty good at dancing, they have a natural sense of rhythm.'

It transpires quickly that Sue is quoting remarks she heard around her from other parents during the show. Sue begins to sob as she says that she and Patricia have been let down by the school and that she believes her precious daughter has no future, anyway in this part of England. 'Will at least the secondary school she's moving be the right place for her?' she asks. James and the head have no idea. They stand there speechless. Sue continues to sob.

Heart stopping moments

After the play the actors remained in role so they could take questions from members of the audience. Then members of the audience jotted down their most vivid memories, including the following:

- When Patricia felt that she was totally alone, deserted even by her own mother

- But then, a few seconds later, the expression of the mother's love for her daughter and her determination to stand by her

- The mother's use of the word nigger and the devastating shock this caused throughout the audience

- The headteacher fidgeting with the bell when he should have been giving James his full attention

- Shivers through the audience when the head referred to 'that coloured kid' and showed also in other ways (for example his casual endorsement of an infamous remark by the Home Secretary) that he was uninterested and insensitive

- The head giving no support or guidance to the class teacher

- The class teacher jumping to a conclusion and then refusing to listen to Patricia's story

- The class teacher's inability to use the word racism until pressed (repeatedly!) by the audience to do so

- Later, the teacher's pain when he finally realised he didn't have an easy answer

- Patricia's mounting frustration when the teacher wouldn't listen to her

- That Patricia and her mum were so used to having to put up with racism in their neighbourhood

- Kerry defending her friend Pat to the hilt, and her account of what adults in her family say when she challenges them about racism – 'they go "yeah, yeah, yeah", they say I'm just a kid, which I am, but I know stuff they don't'

- The despair of the mother at the end.

Points arising

Members of the audience mentioned the following points they would like to consider and discuss further:

- The differences between bullying and racism – in what respects, exactly, are they different and in what respects are they similar? How should each be tackled?

- Language, semantics and political correctness – the importance of using language that is not offensive, but also uncertainty and embarrassment when one is not confident that one has kept up with changing views of appropriate language

- How to develop awareness of cultural diversity in a place like this town, where even a trip to Derby is a major event

- The need to recognise the fears and sense of dispossession of white people in areas of social deprivation and poverty

- How to respond as a white person when another white person makes a racist remark, taking for granted that you will agree with it

- How to respond when a pupil makes a racist or xenophobic (for example, anti-German) remark in the classroom, and how to find out what colleagues do and say at such times, and how to have a uniform approach; and generally, how to deal with prejudices against anyone perceived to be different

- The need to define racism – what is it exactly that we're talking about?

- Whether focusing on racism can cause more problems than it solves

- How to get reliable advice when planning a new venture, so that your best intentions don't backfire

- How to find out whether pupils from minority backgrounds at your school, and their parents, have had negative experiences similar to those of Patricia and her mum

- How a school can engage on issues of racism with parents and the local community.

It is in order to help schools ask, discuss and answer such questions that this handbook has been compiled.

Action plans

Members of the audience were asked to jot notes on the practical implications of the play (a) for themselves as individuals and (b) for their schools.

With regard to personal implications, a recurring reference was to the need to listen to pupils before jumping to conclusions and the need to deal with incidents when they arise, not smooth them over, or sweep them under the carpet. Several participants also mentioned that the presentation had sensitised them to issues of appropriate and inappropriate language.

With regard to action at school-level the following proposals were made:

Anti-bullying policy and practice

- Review the school's written policy on bullying, to make sure that it refers explicitly to racism and that it explains the differences as well as the similarities between bullying and racism

- Find out students' and pupils' view on issues of racism, for example through an anonymous questionnaire

- Hold staff discussions of real or imaginary incidents in order to come towards a common mind on what the key issues and principles are, and a consistent approach when dealing with incidents

- Involve all staff in the review and discussions, not teaching staff only – in particular mid-day supervisors must be involved

- Involve also parents and the local community, so that there is a sense of shared decision-making

- Do all this now – don't wait until a problem arises!

Curriculum

- Move towards staff consensus on key principles and ideas that can and should be taught in all subjects

- Identify positive activities that can be undertaken in each curriculum subject or area

- Audit curriculum materials in current use, and add to them as necessary to ensure that they reflect Britain as a culturally diverse society

- Review, expand and improve the PSHE programme

- Ensure liaison with other cluster schools on curricular issues, as also across departments and areas in each separate school

- Invite in positive role models, for example poets, storytellers and artists.

Drama

- Use the techniques of forum theatre with pupils

- Obtain training for staff in the techniques and principles of forum theatre

- Provide presentations for parents as well as for pupils and students

Links with other schools

- Set up exchanges or contacts with schools in other countries and/or in Derby City

Special days

- Organise a multicultural or international day

Policy documentation

- Make sure that policy documentation is provided for all staff

- Staff to sign or initial a record to confirm that they have read it.

Support from the LEA

- For most or all of the measures listed above, seek moral and institutional support from the LEA, and financial support if available.

And finally

- Make sure these issues don't get shelved!

This handbook

This handbook is a resource for schools as they engage in the tasks listed on the opposite page. In particular it is concerned with the curriculum. Chapter 2 considers the overarching themes and big ideas that should permeate every subject. Chapter 3 discusses each separate subject or curriculum area. Chapter 4 consists of a set of auditing forms, to help schools review their current practice and to make plans for the future. Chapter 5 gives guidance on dealing with racist incidents. Chapter 6 draws threads together from previous chapters in order to support the creation and development of formal policies.

Throughout, the concern is to help make issues of belonging, identity and equality part of the air that staff, children and young people breathe. Or, in the words of the song adopted as the title for a student website, to put them – and to keep them – here, there and everywhere.

Three principles

Running throughout the pages of this book there are three fundamental concerns – belonging, identity and equality. The three go together like, in that famous traditional metaphor, the three legs of a three-legged stool. Take any one of them away and you have lost the use of the other two as well. These concerns are summarised below.

The three key ideas of belonging, identity and equality should underpin not only the formal curriculum but also what is taught and learnt incidentally and implicitly – the hidden curriculum. They should affect:

- the examples, materials and cultural reference points that are used to illustrate abstract ideas in history, geography and the sciences

- the texts, activities, materials and assignments that are used in skill-based subjects, for example ICT, design and technology, literacy and numeracy

- the stories, subjects and situations explored in art, dance, drama, literature and music

- the visual environment of a school – displays, exhibitions, signs and illustrations in classrooms and public areas

- the use of visiting speakers, artists, musicians and storytellers

- the content of assemblies and collective worship

- journeys and visits to places of interest

- fund-raising for charities

- involvement in national projects

Three philosophical principles

Belonging

It is important that all pupils should feel that they belong – to the school itself, to the neighbourhood and locality, and to Britain more generally. Belonging involves shared stories and symbols; a shared sense of having a stake in the well-being and future development of the wider community; and a sense that one is accepted and welcomed, and is able and encouraged to participate and contribute.

Identity

Significant differences of culture, outlook, narrative and experience should be recognised and respected. For example, and particularly obviously, it is unjust to treat girls as if they are boys, and vice versa, or to treat pupils new to English as if they are in fact fluent speakers of English already. But also in many other ways pupils' identities and experiences should be recognised and given respect.

Equality

All pupils are of equal value and should have equal opportunities to learn and to be successful. In this sense, they should all be treated the same and schools should be proactive in removing barriers to learning and success. The philosophical principle of equality is enshrined in national legislation, particularly the Race Relations Act 1976 and the Race Relations Amendment Act 2000, and in international human rights standards.

Source: Derbyshire Education Authority, 2003.

- links with schools in other countries or other parts of Britain
- casual comments and conversations.

This opening chapter ends with a case study from Highfields School, Matlock, and its partner primary schools. It refers to a production of *Sticks, Stones and Macpherson* and to the *Here, There and Everywhere* website. Further, it mentions the practical projects and activities in schools for which this handbook is a resource.

Acknowledgements

The members of the committee of headteachers, teachers and others who advised on the content and revision of Derbyshire's preliminary guidance papers on race equality in schools were Margaret Cadman, Kate Fox, Gill Hutton, Jenny Kiharai-Boyd, Mike Pomerantz, Margaret Stirling, Colin Tucker and Carolyn Wood. The committee was convened, chaired and administered on behalf of Derbyshire Advisory and Inspection Service by Steve Ford. The schools or services represented were Bennerley Fields, Ilkeston; Langley Infants, Heanor; Long Row Primary, Belper; Pottery Primary, Belper; the Schools Psychological Service; and Wilsthorpe Community School, Long Eaton.

The case study from Highfields School and its partner primary schools appears also in *Aiming High: understanding the needs of minority ethnic pupils in mainly white schools*, published by the Department for Education and Skills in summer 2004.

Here, There and Everywhere
– part of the air children breathe

At Highfields School, Matlock, Derbyshire, 1.8 per cent of the students are of minority ethnic background, up from 0.2 per cent a few years ago. It has thirteen partner primary schools. Recently finance became available from the LEA for a continuing professional training day involving all teachers in the partnership. The headteachers resolved that the whole day should be on cultural diversity and arranged for the centrepiece of the event to be a piece of forum theatre presented by a professional company from London. The story was about street racism and playground racism in a mainly white town such as Matlock, and about teacher attitudes and staffroom cultures in the schools in such towns.

The day had a great impact on staff in all fourteen schools and gave impetus and context to a range of projects and activities, including:

- the development of policy statements on cultural diversity for all schools in the area

- reviews of displays and visual environments – diversity, it was said, should be 'part of the air children breathe'

- the incorporation of cultural diversity themes in projects such as the Healthy Schools Programme

- a partnership with inner-city schools in Derby, some 20 miles away, funded by Barclays New Futures: activities include drama, dance and music days for participating primary schools; a website run jointly by Year 11 students; and a commemorative magazine for all those taking part.

2 WHAT'S THE BIG IDEA?
- principles and concepts across the curriculum

Summary

'What's the big idea?' This a key question in curriculum planning – what are the essential generalisations we intend to present and to communicate, the key concepts we want learners to understand and make their own? In this chapter there are notes on six sets of big ideas, as listed below. The ideas are connected to each other and overlap but can be separated and given names, for the sake of convenience. Readers and users of this handbook are invited to formulate their own lists of big ideas, and to compare and contrast their own thoughts with those that are suggested here.

Each set of ideas in this chapter is introduced with a few summarising lines. There is then a commentary illustrated by quotations which have the generic title of 'Views and voices'. These are intended to enrich and extend the commentary as well as to illustrate it and can be used in staff training sessions. Many are vivid and concrete, and some are simple enough to share with pupils and students, particularly in secondary schools.

Shared humanity

Summary

Human beings belong to a single race, the human race. At all times in history and in all cultural traditions, they have certain basic tasks, problems, aspirations and needs in common – there is a shared humanity. Because all have the same underlying humanity, all should be treated fairly and all should have the same basic human rights.

Commentary

An influential curriculum project, *Man – a course of study* developed in the 1960s by Jerome Bruner and his associates, proposed that the following five objectives should underpin all teaching of history, geography and social studies:

- to give our pupils respect for and confidence in the powers of their own minds

- to extend that respect and confidence to their power to think about the human condition, humankind's plight and humankind's social life

- to provide a set of workable models that make it simpler to analyse the nature of the social world in which we live and the condition in which humankind currently is

- to impart a sense of respect for the capacities and humanity of humankind as a species

- to leave the learner with a sense of the unfinished business of human evolution.

Bruner's list continues to be an inspiring summary of educational aims. Aspects of it are relevant for all curriculum areas, not social studies subjects only. Science, mathematics and technology, for example, are concerned with principles and constants that exist independently of specific cultural contexts and they are centrally concerned with 'the unfinished business of human evolution'.

Also, all the visual, literary and performing arts invite reflection on human nature and on the recurring desires, needs and concerns that all human beings have in common, regardless of the stage in human evolution they happen to live in.

Views and voices – 1

Wild with the joy of it

It's 21 July 1969, late evening. Mala is almost 12 years old and lives in London. She's at a party for adult members of her family and this evening they have put the household's TV in the small garden at the back of the house.

Around midnight, tired and bored, I wandered outside again and saw those magical words on the screen. *Man has landed on the moon.* I read them again and again. *Man has landed on the moon. Man has landed on the moon. MAN HAS LANDED ON THE MOON.*

For that millisecond, as the enormity of it sank in, and before I ran inside screeching with excitement, my heart stopped. The memory brings a lump to my throat even now. Because science was so fresh to me, and everything from the clothes we wore to the music we played to the cars we drove was about pushing ideas to their limits. Each new achievement moved me. I was wild with the joy of it! And the adults were too. They streamed out into the yard and we all just stared at the screen, filled with wonder.

Shyama Perera, *One Small Step*, 2004

Views and voices – 2

Precious and beautiful

In strength the human being is no match for the tiger; in speed he can be outstripped by the gazelle; as a swimmer his performance is childish compared with that of a dolphin; his sense of smell is far less acute than that of a dog; his eyes in the daytime are less serviceable than a hawk's, and at night than those of a cat.

Yet in one major respect he outstrips them all – he is capable of what is known as civilisation. That is not simply a short way of saying that he has invented cooking and weaving, the telephone and the plough, the automobile and the hydrogen bomb. Civilisation involves more than the power to make and use tools, to understand and master the forces of nature.

One of the basic differences between man and animals is his power to stand outside himself. Doubtless the tiger and the eagle are capable of the major forms of experience – love, hate, hunger, lust. But they do not *contemplate* their experience, marvel at it as something precious or beautiful in its own right.

Eric Newton, 1960

Like you

In a poem about a Welsh hill farmer R.S.Thomas evokes someone whose lifestyle and daily circumstances are entirely different from those of most of his readers. But underlying the differences of situation and daily life, there is a shared humanity:

> The dirt is under my cracked nails
> The tale of my life is smirched with dung
> The phlegm rattles. But what I am saying
> Over the grasses wet with dew
> Is Listen, listen, I am a man like you.

There is a similar sense of common humanity underlying differences of culture and daily circumstances in an anthology of short stories for teenagers published in 2004. An extract from the editor's introduction appears in *Views and Voices 3*.

Views and voices – 3

Resonate

This collection will, I hope, offer all readers stories that will both resonate with their own experiences and open up windows on to less familiar worlds.

You will meet Asha, who tries to reconcile the pressures of her strict father with her desperate desire to get in with the cool crowd at school; Dilip, whose passion for playing the drums offers him an escape from the warring gangs that rule his estate; Shah Bano, who has a huge crush on her brother's best friend, Feroze, but can't understand his decision to join the army; and Murad, who learns that to love Tsuru he must let her keep her secrets.

You will find hard-hitting stories of domestic violence and the bleak realities of war; and hopeful stories in which a second and third generation of young British Asians meet the challenges of growing up in more than one culture with energy and humour – and discover both the complexity and richness of experience that this can bring.

Rehana Ahmed, Introduction to *Walking a Tightrope*, 2004

Human rights and human differences

It is because all human beings share the same basic humanity that all should be treated equally – all should have the same basic human rights. 'The time will come,' Anne Frank wrote in her diary, 'when we'll be people again, and not just Jews.' Her longing was that she and her family should be recognised as human beings – members of the human species – and treated accordingly by wider society. To be as 'just a Jew' was to be treated as less than human.

Views and voices – 4

People again

The time will come when we'll be people again and not just Jews.

Anne Frank, 11 April 1944

Anne's diary showed vividly that she was certainly not 'just a Jew'. She had feelings, dreams, worries, passions, loves, angers and hopes in common with all other teenagers. The diary showed too, however, that Jewishness was a fundamental feature of her identity. In the same way, every human being belongs to a home, a tradition, a culture, a story. In consequence, being different from most other people in terms of where one belongs is a fundamental and inescapable part of being human. To be human is to be different. Respect for human rights includes, amongst other things, respect for difference and recognition of positive human needs for belonging and identity. There is further discussion of this point overleaf. On later pages (see pages 16-17) there is discussion of justice and human rights.

Across the curriculum

Art, drama, history, music, novels, poetry, religion and stories all explore humankind's basic humanity. In science, pupils learn about aspects of human biology that are universal, about universals in the inorganic world and about science as a universal human activity. Universals in biology are also encountered in health education and PE. In geography, pupils learn about recurring patterns in relationships between human beings and their physical environment.

Difference and identity

Summary

Through history and across the world, and within each society, there are different ways of pursuing the same values and human needs. The principal differences are to do with gender, culture, class, nation, religion, ethnicity, language and status. Every individual belongs to a range of different groups, and therefore has a range of different belongings. Also, and partly in consequence, all individuals change and develop. Children and young people need to feel confident in their own identity but also to be open to change and development, and to be able to engage positively with other identities.

Commentary

Addressing Edgar, living in a cave like a wild beast, King Lear in Shakespeare's play exclaims: 'Thou art the thing itself; unaccommodated man is no more but such a poor, bare, forked animal as thou art.' In context, the words are a moving statement about shared humanity beneath surface differences of clothing, rank and status.

Lear's famous words are misleading, however, if they are taken to mean that human beings ever exist outside cultural and social locations, and therefore outside situations and relationships of unequal power, and outside historical circumstances. No one is totally unaccommodated – or, for that, matter, unaccommodating. On the contrary, everyone is embedded in a cultural tradition and in a period of history, and in a system of unequal power relations. Rowan Williams, the Archbishop of Canterbury, has pointed out that the claim that all human are 'the same under the skin' is a dangerous over-simplification, for 'the only humanity we have is one that is bound up in difference'. (See *Views and voices* 5.)

Belonging to Britain

Everyone is different. But also, everyone needs to feel they belong. Virtually all pupils currently in British schools will spend the rest of their lives in Britain. It is important therefore that they should feel that they belong here and that Britain belongs to them. In this sense Britishness should be an important part,

---

Views and voices – 5

Bound up in difference

The liberal assumption that 'treating everyone alike' is the answer rests on a view of human nature which is deeply problematic. It assumes that there is a basic 'inner' humanity, beyond flesh and skin pigmentation and history and conflict, which is the same for all people. But human existence is precisely life that is lived in speech and relation, and so in history – what we share as humans is not a human 'essence' outside history, but a common involvement in the limits and relativities of history. The only humanity we have is one that is bound up in difference, in the encounter of physical and linguistic strangers.

...When great stress is laid upon our oneness 'under the skin', there is always the risk of rendering that as 'this stranger is really the same as me' – which subtly reinforces the dominant group's assumptions of the right to define. The norm is where I or we stand. This risk is one reason for looking very hard at the goal of 'treating everyone alike'. It represents the worthy and correct commitment to avoid discrimination that overtly disadvantages or distances the stranger; but it can fail to see the prior need to allow them to be strangers.

Rowan Williams, 1999

Views and voices – 6

Who we are

Culture has an important part to play in defining and preserving cultural identity – of the individual, of communities, of the nation as a whole. England has a tradition of importing and exporting culture – from Beowulf, via Handel to Vaughan Williams (whose tonality derives from his teaching by Ravel). And today we have the new melding of cultural traditions that is the result of population transfer and globalisation; the acceptable face of globalisation, one might say.

Consider a choreographer like Akram Khan, who is British but draws on both Western and Eastern dance traditions to create something unique. So we are inventing new forms of dance, of music, of drama, that transcend traditional boundaries, and help give us a national identity which is uniquely ours. Culture defines who we are, it defines us as a nation. And only culture can do this.

Tessa Jowell, minister for culture, 2004

A part to play

What can we do to make sure that everyone is able to feel proud to be British and feel they belong to this country?

How can we make sure that people who may not have been born here or whose families have come to live in Britain from other countries don't feel that they have to change their traditions to feel that they belong to Britain?

How can we help people, especially young people, feel that they have a part to play in the future of this country?

Home Office consultation, 2004

though not the only part, of their identity. All need to be comfortable with terms such as Black British, British Muslim and English British and with the fact that there are, and always have been, many different ways of being British.

Promoting a sense of belonging is not necessarily an alternative to recognition of difference. On the contrary, they can and should go hand in hand. This point was central in a consultation exercise on citizenship conducted by the Home Office in 2004. There is an extract from one of the consultation documents in *Views and voices* 7.

Household and wider world

Comparing and contrasting different ways of doing things, and different ways of seeing, viewing and interpreting, is a fundamental human activity. It's

Ask Mummy Ask Daddy

When I ask Daddy
Daddy says ask Mummy

When I ask Mummy
Mummy says ask Daddy.
I don't know where to go.

Better ask my teddy
He never says no.

John Agard, 1985

A foreign place

I find myself returning again and again to a hauntingly beautiful passage by Hugo of St Victor, a twelfth century monk from Saxony:

The person who finds his homeland sweet is still a tender beginner; he to whom every soil is as his native one is already strong; but he is perfect to whom the entire world is as a foreign place.

Erich Auerbach, the great German scholar who spent the years of World War Two as an exile in Turkey, cites this passage as a model for anyone – man and woman – wishing to transcend the restraints of imperial or national or provincial limits. Only through this attitude can a historian, for example, begin to grasp human experience and its written records in all their diversity and particularity.

Edward Said, 1993

important to help pupils see diversity and difference as interesting and exciting, and indeed as necessary and invaluable, rather than as merely confusing and depressing. And to live with diversity within themselves as well as outside. And in their own immediate household as well as the wider world.

The notion of a difference-free world, as John Agard beautifully and so crisply recalls (*Views and voices 8*), is appealing but a fantasy. A similar point about the importance of detachment and independence is made by the authors quoted in *Views and voices 9*.

The references to homeland, foreign soil and entire world in *Views and voices 9* are explored further overleaf.

Across the curriculum

In all subjects, the texts, visual material and electronic resources can reflect the reality that Britain is a multi-ethnic society and is part of an interdependent world. Similarly the tasks, problems and assignments that are set can reflect these aspects of the real world. In many subjects, in addition, there are direct opportunities for teaching and learning about cultural differences, and differences of perception, interpretation and narrative.

Local and global

Summary

Countries, cultures and communities are not cut off from each other. On the contrary, there has been much borrowing, mingling and mutual influence over the centuries between different countries and cultural traditions. Events and trends in one place in the modern world are frequently affected by events and trends elsewhere. You cannot understand your own local world close at hand without seeing it as part of a global system. The global system has a range of interacting sub-systems: ecological, cultural, economic and political. There are benefits, but also dangers and disadvantages.

Commentary

In her autobiographical novel *Lark Rise to Candleford*, set in a tiny hamlet in England in the 1880s, Flora Thompson showed how children in such places at that time saw their locality. There is an extract in *Views and voices 10*.

Flora Thompson describes how the vast majority of human beings in the past, not just children and not just in Britain, lived and thought for most of their days. She also evokes a picture of the world as consisting of concentric circles, with one's own locality at the centre and other countries out on the fringe, as sketched in figure 1.

Figure 1: A customary view of the world.

It is still the case that each person's world close at hand, the one you can see and hear and touch and smell, is 'more than life-size and more richly coloured' when compared with places and events far away, those you have only heard about. It will always be thus. But it is no longer possible to understand your local world unless you see it as belonging to systems much larger than itself – systems in which skylines and national boundaries are largely irrelevant. 'Here' is not only the centre of concentric circles but also where various global systems meet, for example systems of economics, politics, ecology and culture. An alternative picture of the world is sketched in figure 2.

Figure 2: An alternative view of the world

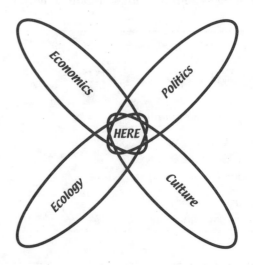

Views and voices – 10

Beyond their world

Beyond their garden in summer were fields of wheat and barley and oats, which sighed and rustled and filled the air with sleepy pollen and earth scents. These fields were large and flat, and stretched away to a distant line of trees set in the hedgerows.

To the children at that time these trees marked the boundary of their world.

Beyond their world enclosed by the trees there was, they were told, a wider world, with other hamlets and villages and towns and the sea and, beyond that, other countries, where people spoke languages different from their own. Their father had told them so.

But they had no mental picture of these, they were but ideas, unrealised: whereas in their own little world within the tree boundary everything appeared to them more than life-size, and more richly coloured.

Flora Thompson, about life in an English village in the 1880s

Views and voices – 11

The football match

There is a tale told of a Martian. This Martian was a scientist. He came to Planet Earth, to do some research on the oceans. He collected samples of seawater.

Before returning to Mars he happened to find himself at a football match. He had never seen football played before. He watched with amazement. How, he wondered, could he possibly understand what was going on. He decided to do the same for football as he had done for the oceans – he would take a sample. So he trained the zoom lens of his camera on just one footballer. He recorded every single movement the player made – every step and leap and breath he took.

Occasionally a round object came close the player's feet and the player would kick it. Occasionally the player would appear to collide with another player. All these events were recorded on the film.

The Martian returned to his laboratory on Mars. He analysed the samples of seawater and published a book on the composition of Planet Earth's oceans. He then examined the film of the football player frame by frame and developed an elaborate and elegant theory about, so he thought, the basic nature of football. He published his findings and – so the story goes – won many awards from his fellow Martians for his distinguished contributions to Martian science.

Source: Centre for World Development Education, 1980

Views and voices – 12

Insecurity, anger and hysteria

As power has shifted to the global level, democracy has withered within national boundaries. Which means that globalisation is experienced as an alien force over which we have no control. And immigrants, as the most obvious manifestation of the new global forces, are easy targets.

In the hothouse of powerlessness, the new racism that is sprouting is based on insecurity, anger and hysteria. It finds support in the suburbs or the countryside as easily as in the inner city. Its main focus is the new migrants to Britain – whether asylum seekers from the Middle East, Asia and Africa, workers from eastern Europe or undocumented migrant workers from outside the West. And Muslims come in for particular hatred... These groups are portrayed as culturally inferior, having nothing of political or cultural value to contribute to the world.

Arun Kundnani, 2004

Systems

It has been suggested that the core concept of system can be explained through the metaphor of a football match, as sketched in *Views and voices 11*. The two goalkeepers in a football match seldom affect each other directly. But both are part of the same game and the actions of neither would be comprehensible if considered in isolation from the overall state of play.

It was in the youth of Flora Thompson's generation that the pace of change began to speed up and within the lifetime of students currently at secondary school that a new word – globalisation – came into widespread use amongst specialists to describe the new situation. Other phrases evoking new types of

connection between the local and the global include spaceship earth, global village, one world and world society.

Globalisation has its beneficial, dynamic and exciting aspects, as recalled in *Views and voices 6*. But it also has negative and disruptive features. It can threaten people's sense of identity and belonging; increase economic inequality between and within countries; weaken the capacity of democratically elected governments to do what is best for those whom they represent; and undermine local languages, traditions and cultures. The insecurities which it causes can be breeding grounds for various kinds of dogmatism, racism and prejudice, as outlined in *Views and voices 12*.

Across the curriculum

Economic interdependence is an essential concept in geography. Ecological interdependence is fundamental in biology and chemistry. Political interdependence is central in all studies of causation in history. Cultural interdependence, involving fusion, cross-over and mutual influences and borrowing, is a recurring feature in art, design, drama, literature, music and technology.

Achievement everywhere

Summary

Examples of high achievement are to be found in a wide range of cultures, societies and traditions, not only in 'the west'. And they are to be found in all areas of human endeavour – the arts and sciences, law and ethics, personal and family life, religion and spirituality, moral and physical courage, invention, politics, imagination.

Commentary

The 'default position' in the curriculum can all too often be the assumption that all significant human achievements arose in the west – this is what is communicated, even though teachers do not consciously intend it. For example, the message illustrated in *Views and voices 13* is presented subliminally, even though no teacher nowadays would express it so bluntly or directly. The book from which the quotation is taken was extremely influential in its time and was reprinted many times. The author explicitly attributes all excellence in the modern world to people with white faces and of 'European stock'.

Views and voices – 13

White men of European stock

It is to European man that the world owes the incomparable gifts of modern science. To the conquest of nature through knowledge the contributions made by Asiatics have been negligible and by Africans (Egyptians excluded) non-existent.

The printing press and the telescope, the steam-engine, the internal combustion engine and the aeroplane, the telegraph and telephone, wireless broadcasting and the cinematograph, the gramophone and television, together with all the leading discoveries in physiology, the circulation of the blood, the laws of respiration and the like, are the result of researches carried out by white men of European stock. It is hardly excessive to say that the material fabric of modern civilised life is the result of the intellectual daring and tenacity of the European peoples.

H.A.L Fisher, 1936

Views and voices – 14

Where was the balance?

I remember the excitement with which I greeted the amazing new world of my secondary school – a place to conquer life's mysteries and storm through the broad corridors of adolescence.

Reality was a little different, however. My newfound world was a singularly white, all boys grammar school where the National Front would be happily distributing leaflets at our school gates and an embittered music teacher would ritualistically prod me out of the music rooms for attempting Indian ragas without a written score. Indian classical music is an oral tradition. I never had the heart to break it to him. So what was I taught? History. Yes, I was taught history. How wonderful an experience it would be, I imagined, to learn the origins of my ancestors – to learn of the Aryan journey to the Indus valley and of the Dravidians' historic migration to south India. How inspiring to hear of the great Moghul empire and origins of the Vedas, the Upanishads and the epic Maharabharata, I thought. What I did learn however was a lot easier to grasp than any of that. Five words: 'India was a British colony.' I had no problem with what I was taught per se...But where was the balance? Where was I in this ambitious picture of world history?

So I went through school with an uneasy suspicion that I was inferior. It may have been a product of the notion that the history of the non-white population of this world is embedded in slavery and colonisation, or perhaps the echoing resonance of the word Paki as it accompanied me through the hostile corridors of the science block.

Still, in a school where the subject of history meant 'History of White Men' and music revolved around Western classical harmony and counterpoint, I guess I emerged fairly well balanced...

Nitin Sawney, 2003

The same the world over

More than once during my days in Hong Kong I heard the view propounded that Western values, democracy, human rights, civil liberties, were incompatible with 'Asian' values. It is an idea I have learnt to reject utterly...Standards of decency matter everywhere – and the aspiration to be treated decently is the same the world over. Freedom and human rights are not Western values only. Is Aung San Suu Kyi in Burma, an inspiration to freedom lovers across the world, not Asian? Looking at my island home from a distance helped me to see our 'Western' values in their proper context.

... As the great Indian economist Amartya Sen has pointed out, when European nations still believed in the divine right of kings, Indian emperors were practising tolerance and defending diversity.

Chris Patten, 2003

The default position has the consequence of marginalising pupils who identify through their families with cultures and communities outside the west, and of miseducating everyone else. The issues are poignantly expressed by the musician Nitin Sawney in *Views and voices 14*. Sawney is of Indian heritage. His recollection of the curriculum at his British school is bound up with memories of racism in the corridors and at the school gates.

As recalled in *Views and voices 13*, the default position about Western superiority is frequently expressed with regard to scientific discovery and invention. Another area is politics and the law. *Views and voices 15* valuably stresses that concern for justice and the rule of law is universal, not a Western value only.

Across the curriculum

In every subject, examples of achievement, invention, creativity, insight and heroism can be taken from a wide range of cultures, both in the present and in the past.

Man, men and people

The influential historian quoted in *Views and voices 13* refers to 'white European man'. Such use of the word man, meaning all humankind, was usual at the time he was writing. Also, however, it is significant. The achievements he was celebrating were associated in his mind with males, not with all people. The invisibility of women in the conventional view of history, as evoked in *Views and voices 13*, is analogous to the invisibility of all continents in the world other than Europe and North America.

The narrator in Carol Shields' novel *Unless* is the mother of three daughters. The eldest daughter has dropped out of college and is living as a down-and-out on the pavements of a nearby city. The mother is devastated by her daughter's action and frets continually about what went wrong, and whether she herself could have avoided this happening, and what the future has in store for her other girls. One day she comes across an advertisement for a set of books entitled Great Minds of the Western Intellectual World. There are portraits of the people in question, all of them men. She writes a long letter to the editor of the magazine where the advertisement has appeared. The letter ends with quiet desperation:

> I realise I cannot influence your advertising policy. My only hope is that my daughter, her name is Norah, will not pick up a copy of the magazine, read this page, and understand, as I have for the first time, how casually and completely she is shut out of the universe. I have two other daughters too – Christine, Natalie – and I worry about them both. All the time.

Shields poignantly criticises any curriculum that 'casually and completely' shuts many pupils 'out of the universe'. Her remarks are relevant to a wide range of issues of belonging, identity and equality, not to gender issues only.

Conflict, justice and rights

Summary

In all societies and situations – including families, schools, villages, nations, the world – there are disagreements and conflicts of interest. In consequence there is a never-ending need to construct, and to keep in good repair, rules, laws, customs and systems that all people accept as reasonable and fair.

Commentary

Over the centuries philosophers and political theorists have argued at length and in depth about what the features are of a just community. Also, children from an early age have a keen interest in justice and a robust sense of what is and is not fair. In *Great Expectations* Dickens observed that 'in the little world in which children have their existence, there is nothing so finely perceived and so finely felt as injustice.' There is a fuller quotation in *Views and voices 16*.

An influential theory of justice has been developed by the American philosopher John Rawls. What kind of society would human beings devise, he asks, if they did not know what their position in that society would be? Rawls's theory has been put into various accessible forms for children and young people. One such attempt to explain his ideas is touched on in *Views and voices 17*. The writer imagines that it is the year 3136. A starship is on its way from earth to colonise a distant planet. Despite advances in

---

Views and voices – 16

The smart without a name

The narrator recalls an event when he was about eight years old.

... I was so humiliated, hurt, spurned, offended, angry, sorry – I cannot hit on the right term for the smart – God knows what its name was – that tears started to my eyes.

... I looked about me for a place to hide my face in, and got behind one of the gates in the brewery-lane, and leaned my sleeve against the wall there, and leaned my forehead on it, and cried. As I cried, I kicked the wall, and took a hard twist at my hair; so bitter were my feelings, and so sharp was the smart without a name.

...'In the little world in which children have their existence, there is nothing so finely perceived and so finely felt as injustice. It may be only small injustice that the child can be exposed to; but the child is small, and its world is small, and its rocking-horse stands as many hands high, according to scale, as a big-boned Irish hunter. Within myself I had sustained, from my babyhood, a perpetual conflict with injustice. I had known, from the time I could speak, that my sister, in her capricious and violent coercion, was unjust to me.

From *Great Expectations* by Charles Dickens, set in about 1820

Views and voices – 17

The worth of each individual

From their general understanding of psychology, the passengers know that to follow their aim in life with vigour and delight they will need a basic self-confidence in their own worth as persons, a sense of relf-respect. Self-respect depends to a considerable degree on the respect of others. Unless someone else values and upholds the worthwhileness of my aims, it will be extremely difficult for me to carry on believing they are worthwhile. The passengers will probably therefore agree that the principles they draw up must be based on mutual respect. It is in their rational self-interest to have a society which shows respect for the dignity and worth of each individual person.

... If I am among the passengers, I shall want an agreement which I can reasonably expect to honour in the worst possible circumstances. The society I help build must be capable of inspiring the willing cooperation of all its members, including the poorest, weakest and least naturally gifted – who might well include myself.

Thus, if I am a passenger on that starship, my reasoning will almost certainly lead me to one conclusion: Whatever else I agree to about our new society I must make sure that I could accept being one of its weakest or least fortunate members.

Brian Wren, 1977

Seeing and approaching the other

In summary, the distinctions between closed and open views of the other are to do with:

whether the other is seen as monolithic, static and authoritarian, or as diverse and dynamic with substantial internal debates

whether the other is seen as totally different and separate, or as both similar and interdependent, sharing a common humanity and a common space

whether the other is seen as inferior, backward and primitive compared with one's own group, or as different but equal

whether the other is seen as an aggressive enemy to be feared, opposed and defeated, or as a cooperative partner with whom to work on shared problems, locally, nationally and internationally

whether others are seen as manipulative, devious and self-righteous in their beliefs, or as sincere and genuine

whether criticisms made by the other of one's own group are rejected out of hand or are considered and debated

whether double standards are applied in descriptions and criticisms of the other and one's own group, or whether criticisms are even-handed

whether negative generalisations about the other are seen as natural and 'common sense', or as problematic and to be challenged.

Commission on the Future of Multi-Ethnic Britain, 2000

astrophysics and space technology, the journey will take several generations of earth time. To prevent ageing, the passengers are put into a kind of hibernation. They can think and talk but all have totally forgotten, for the duration of the journey, their name, gender, ethnicity, class, status, income, age, level of intelligence, personality traits, religious and political attitudes, and physical attractiveness.

The condition of space hibernation means that everyone is in a cocoon, and cannot even debate with others, let alone form coalitions and majorities. *Views and voices 17* comments on their probable conclusions.

Rawls and his followers maintain that the kind of society to emerge from considerations such as those sketched in *Views and voices 17* would insist on equal opportunities with regard to ethnicity, gender, disability, religion, sexuality and age and would observe international human rights standards.

Further, there would need to be agreement about rules and procedures for debate and the handling of disagreements. In this connection it would be necessary to distinguish between 'open' views of people with whom one disagrees and 'closed'. The distinction has been explained by the Commission on Multi-Ethnic Britain as shown in *Views and voices 18*. It is rather abstract but has many practical implications for how the curriculum of schools handles issues to do with equal opportunities and human rights, and about the resolution of conflict.

Across the curriculum

It is particularly in history, PSHE and citizenship education that social and political concepts to do with conflict resolution and justice are taught and developed directly. Indirectly, they can be a dimension in all subjects, particularly literature and stories and the creative and performing arts.

Race and racisms

Summary

All human beings belong to the same species – there is a single human race. However, there is a widespread belief that differences in physical appearance are significant, particularly with regard to skin colour, and that physical appearance is a reliable sign of who belongs in a society and who does not. In the past it was falsely believed by white people that they were superior to not-white people and this belief was used to justify domination, exploitation and enslavement. Although false, the belief exercised a powerful influence and still persists. Beliefs about belonging and superiority are expressed indirectly through practices, behaviour and systems as well directly in words.

Commentary

The United Nations World Conference Against Racism (WCAR) in 2001 summarised its concerns with the phrase 'racism, racial discrimination, xenophobia and related intolerance'. The equivalent phrase used by the Council of Europe is 'racism, xenophobia, antisemitism and intolerance'. Both phrases are cumbersome, but valuably signal that there is a complex cluster of matters to be addressed. The single word 'racism', as customarily used, does not encompass them all.

In effect the WCAR argued that the term racism should be expanded to refer to a wide range of intolerance, not just to intolerance where the principal marker of difference is physical appearance and skin colour. For example, the term should encompass patterns of prejudice and discrimination such as antisemitism and sectarianism, where the markers of supposed difference are religious and cultural rather than to do with physical appearance. The plural term 'racisms' is sometimes used to evoke this point.

Racism takes different forms according to who the victims are and what their characteristics are believed to be. For example, anti-Black racism is different from anti-Asian racism, and both are different from anti-Muslim racism, also known as Islamophobia. Anti-Irish racism must be recognised as a significant factor in the history of the British Isles, as also racism directed against Gypsies and Travellers. Latterly, there has emerged in Britain and Ireland, and indeed throughout western Europe, a set of phenomena known as anti-refugee racism or xeno-racism. It is described in *Views and voices 12*.

Biological and cultural

In nearly every kind of racism there is both a biological and a cultural strand but the strands appear in different combinations at different times and in different places. The biological one uses physical features of supposed difference, particularly skin colour and facial features, to recognise 'the other'. The cultural strand refers to differences of religion, language and way of life. Both strands involve believing that certain differences amongst human beings are fixed as well as significant, can justify unjust distributions of power and resources, and can determine who is and who is not a full or real member of the national society.

Views and voices – 19

My badge of identity

'You've been blessed with brains, Mala,' Ma would say.

'But if I'm really that clever, why do you keep repeating everything as if I can't remember from the last time?'

'In this country you are nothing. Just a coloured face with no status. You have to go out and earn it.'

'Everyone has to go out and earn it.'

'But it's harder for you.'

I hated that. It made me feel like I had a disability or a hideous disfigurement that made me less capable of achievement. It was like she too was finding things wrong with our brown skin instead of telling the racists to bugger off.

My skin was my badge of identity: a declaration of my history and culture. An additional point in the game of success. I thought everything about me was terrific... But Ma was experiencing life on the periphery of British society with people who considered her 'other'. I was growing up alongside those people, and if they were sometimes rude or ignorant I just put them right. I saw myself absolutely as their equal, their colleague – and, usually, their friend.

Shyama Perera, *One Small Step*, 2004

The distinction is sometimes said to be between 'colour racism' and 'cultural racism', or between North-South racism and West-East racism. Such phrases have their uses, but obscure the reality that physical and cultural markers are usually combined. Since 11 September 2001, issues of culture and religion have become even more salient than they were before.

It is important to avoid the implication that Asian, black and other minority ethnic people in Britain are passive victims of racism, waiting for white people to come to their assistance. The reality is that they have substantial personal and cultural resources for withstanding racism and with which to contribute powerfully to British society. This point is well expressed in *Views and voices 19* and *Views and voices 20*.

Institutional racism and street racism

A further distinction has to be drawn between 'institutional racism' and 'street racism'. Another formulation of this distinction refers to 'the racism that discriminates' and 'the racism that kills'. A solution to the one is seldom a solution to the other – though these two forms of racism are certainly connected in various ways, not two entirely different beasts. In schools, 'playground racism' is the equivalent of street racism. There is fuller discussion in chapter 5.

The term institutional racism was coined in the United States in the 1960s, and became widely known in Britain following the publication of the Stephen Lawrence Inquiry report in 1999. In its oral submission to the Inquiry the Black Police Association pointed out that institutional racism has two aspects: the 'net effects' of an organisation on the one hand and its occupational culture on the other. The forum theatre presentation *Sticks, Stones and Macpherson*, described in chapter 1 is about institutional racism in staffroom culture as well as about playground racism as experienced by Patricia, and street racism experienced by her parents.

Views and voices – 20

Within their hearts a dream

Fifty years ago the SS Empire Windrush dropped anchor at Tilbury docks and discharged 492 Jamaicans. It is these individuals, and a quarter of a million who succeeded them, who deserve our acknowledgement, respect and gratitude, for as they stood on the deck of the ship and stared out at the white cliffs of Dover, they carried within their hearts a dream. And like all great pioneers, in the face of much adversity and innumerable obstacles, they remained true to their dream. Without them Britain would be a poorer place.

Caryl Phillips, 2001

Pupils need also to know about strategies, actions and campaigns to prevent and address racism, locally, nationally and internationally; equal opportunities in employment and the provision of services; the role of legislation; conflict, and the management and resolution of conflict; intercultural communication and relationships; and justice and fairness.

And, not least, they need to know what they themselves can do to address racism within their own sphere of influence.

Across the curriculum

It is particularly in history, PSHE and citizenship education that social and political concepts to do with race and racisms are taught and developed directly. Indirectly, they can be a dimension in all subjects, particularly literature and stories and the creative and performing arts. In science, opportunities can be taken to stress that there is a single human species.

3 PLACES AND SPACES
opportunities and openings in each subject

This chapter considers each curriculum subject or area in turn. In each instance there is a discussion of general principles and this is accompanied by practical examples, notes on opportunities within national schemes of work and evocative quotations. The discussions and examples are consistent with, but frequently go further than, legislative requirements and expectations, for example those that are reflected in England by the National Curriculum programmes of study, the Qualifications and Curriculum Authority (QCA) schemes of work, the national literacy strategy and the national numeracy strategy.

Art and design

Overview

Art and design has two aspects:

- developing skills of representation and expression
- study and appreciation of work by others.

The subject is therefore relevant to the big ideas and key concepts outlined in the previous chapter when:

- in their own expressive work learners have opportunities to explore issues of personal and cultural identity, shared humanity, difference, diversity, conflict and justice
- in the study and appreciation of art and design created by others, attention is drawn to the ways artists have handled issues of personal and cultural identity, shared humanity, difference, diversity, conflict and justice
- the art and design created by others is selected from a wide range of cultural and artistic traditions and shows ways in which artists working in different traditions influence and inspire each other
- displays in the school foyer and other public spaces reflect and foster a diverse but inclusive school community.

Great art is inherently ambiguous and unfathomable and therefore promotes 'negative capability' – being happy, in Keats's famous words, to be ' in uncertainties, mysteries, doubts, without any irritable reaching after fact and reason'. It is a quality required by all the themes discussed in chapter 2.

Views and voices – 21

I often paint fakes

There was once a spate on the market of fake Picassos. An art dealer acquired what he knew to be a genuine Picasso and took it to the artist to obtain a certificate of authentification. Picasso looked at the painting and said he couldn't provide a certificate, for the painting was a fake. 'But señor, I saw you paint this picture with my own eyes.' – 'So what,' said Picasso. 'I often paint fakes.'

Arthur Koestler, 1963

Commentary

National requirements relevant to the principles and concepts outlined in chapter 2 include the following. Learners should:

- respond to personal, social, cultural and environmental issues within the broad themes of *themselves and their experiences* and *natural and made objects and environments*
- use a variety of methods and approaches to communicate observations, ideas and feelings and design and make images and artefacts
- develop knowledge of codes and conventions in art, craft and design and how these are used to represent ideas, beliefs and values.

These requirements provide a sound basis for exploring issues of personal and cultural identity, and issues of conflict, justice and equality in wider society. Also, even more fundamentally, they invite reflection on human nature and creativity, on differing perspectives and points of view, and on the features and purposes of art.

Views and voices – 22

Belief in life

The West Riding of Yorkshire is a producer country – a land of grim and wonderful contrasts where men and women seemed to me, as a child, very tender and exceedingly strong in their belief in life. It is a country of quite extraordinary natural beauty and grandeur: and the contrast of this natural order with the unnatural disorder of the towns, the slag heaps, the dirt and ugliness, made my respect and love for men and women all the greater. For the dignity and kindliness of colliers, mill hands, steel – all the people who made up that great industrial area – gave me a lasting belief in the unity of man with nature, the nature of hills and dales beyond the towns. It is upon this unity that our continued existence depends.

Barbara Hepworth, 1980

There is a recurring requirement in the national curriculum that art and design should draw on a diversity of traditions, and should explore borrowings, interactions and mutual influences between different traditions. Learners should:

Review and development

On page 52, ten features of good practice in art and design are listed in order to guide reviews of current provision, and to assist with planning further developments.

Views and voices – 23

Any multicultural society

She draws on her own experience and thoughts within the framework of a duality of culture (British/Muslim) to explore the often complex nature of these cultures in relation not only to each other but also, vitally, to herself. Her own cultural background of having been raised within the Islamic faith to parents who migrated to Britain some forty years ago forms the basis of much of her work, raising issues of her own sense of cultural identity. Although her work stems from a very personal sense of being, she is aware that it also encompasses broader concerns in any multicultural society today.

... Her family are a constant source of inspiration and often their oral histories feed into each work. Her recent pieces juxtapose her practice as an artist, employing elements of figuration within her creative process, with the non-representational conventions of art-making from her Islamic heritage.

From a leaflet about *Hybrid Visions*, an exhibition by Sophia Shamim, Midlands Arts Centre, summer 2004

- engage with contemporary art, craft and design in a variety of genres, styles and traditions

- understand the role and function of art, craft and design in different times and cultures

- assess visual and other information, including images and artefacts from different historical, social and cultural contexts

- understand continuity and change in the purposes of artists, craftspeople and designers from Western Europe and the wider world.

Skills of criticism, both of one's own work and of that of others, are fundamental. Learners should:

- evaluate critically the work of artists, craftspeople and designers and apply their learning in the context of their own ideas, methods and approaches.

- reflect on, adapt and improve their own work and make independent choices and decisions about its purpose and meanings

- identify what they might change in their current work or develop in their future work.

Schemes of work

QCA schemes of work particularly relevant to the big ideas and key concepts discussed in chapter 2 include *Self-portrait; Mother nature, designer; Can we change places?; Viewpoints; People in action; A sense of place; Self-image; Life events; Personal places, public spaces; Visiting a museum, gallery or site.*

Classroom examples

Viewpoints

Learners investigate and draw objects and artefacts from a range of cultural settings and from different viewpoints; they use charcoal, chalk, clay, paints, inks, crayons and pencils.

Everyday life

Learners compare and contrast depictions of everyday life in Egyptian wall paintings, Greek vases, the Bayeux Tapestry, Indian miniatures, Japanese and Chinese art, Breughel the Elder, modern photography, advertisements, family snapshots and archive photographs. They create images of their own daily life and of life in their community and neighbourhood, using some of the same methods and approaches.

The local community

Learners use a range of media, including photographs, video, computer graphics and installations, to explore and express views and feelings about their local community and their own identity within it.

Posters

Learners examine and discuss a collection of posters and publicity material on themes such as sustainable development, equal opportunities, respect for the disabled, racial justice and human rights. They establish criteria for evaluation of such posters with regard to colour, composition, shape, font and format in the lettering, register of language, and images and assumptions relating to people and situations. They design and create their own posters.

Fusion

Learners study the principal international influences on Picasso and other artists of the last 100 years and the ways their work represents fusion of a range of traditions, cultures and genres. Learners then create their own work, similarly drawing on a range of genres and traditions.

Citizenship

Overview

It is in citizenship education and in personal, social and health education (PSHE) that the ideas and concepts discussed in chapter 2 are most likely to be taught directly. There can be recurring emphasis, in every aspect of citizenship education, on shared humanity; difference, belonging and identity; achievements and excellence in many different settings and contexts; the local neighbourhood and its links with global systems; rights, conflict, justice and fairness; and race, racisms and racial justice.

Concepts and skills of citizenship are taught and learnt not only directly but also implicitly through the ways in which schools and classrooms are organised. Also, as discussed in other parts of this chapter, they can feature in all other curriculum subjects. For example, as stressed in *Views and voices 24*, they are fundamental in the teaching of history.

Views and voices – 24

Ordinary act

Arguing with the past, like paying taxes, like observing the law, like queuing, like not playing music full blast when others will be disturbed, has suddenly become a vital part of being a member of society, an ordinary but important act of citizenship, a factor in establishing the idea of a home as a place you would like to belong, and might be allowed to stay.

Marina Warner, 1994

Commentary

In programmes of citizenship education, learners develop knowledge and understanding of:

- their own neighbourhood and community, its history, groupings and sense of identity, and current issues of concern

- the origins and changing nature of diverse identities in the United Kingdom, including national (English, Irish, Scottish, Welsh), regional, religious including British Muslim), and ethnic (including black British, British Asian)

- the ways in which Britain is, and always has been, interdependent with the wider world – economic, cultural, political and ecological

- the world as a global community and the need for supra-national debate and decision-making

on issues of shared concern such as sustainable development, the management of conflict and protection of human rights; the role of the European Union, the Commonwealth and the United Nations

- the nature and consequences of racisms in society, including Islamophobia, and of racist teasing, bullying and aggressive behaviour in learners' own experience; how to challenge racist incidents; the role of law and equal opportunities legislation; campaigns, projects, movements and struggles for racial justice.

With regard to skills, students are expected to:

- justify orally and in writing personal opinions about issues, problems and events, and to contribute to exploratory discussions and debates, showing respect for opinions with which one disagrees.

- use their imagination to consider other people's experiences and think about, express, explain and critically evaluate views that are not one's own.

- challenge offensive behaviour, prejudice, bullying, racism and discrimination assertively; to take the initiative in giving and receiving support; to help mediate in disputes amongst peers.

- consider critically how the media present information.

With regard to attitudes and values, students are expected to develop:

- pride in their own identity and in communities to which they belong

- readiniess to look critically at the communities to which they belong, and to contribute positively to change and development

- attitudes of curiosity, openness and generosity towards others.

The relevance of the performing, literary and visual arts to citizenship education is evoked in *Views and voices 25*.

Picturing Britain

The picture of Britain as a 92/8 society – where ninety-two per cent are said to belong to one vast majority since they are white and eight per cent to

---

Review and development

On page 53, ten features of good practice in citizenship education are listed in order to guide reviews of current provision and to assist with planning future developments.

Views and voices – 25

Starch in our backbones

Our singers, composers and musicians must be encouraged to sing the song of struggle, the song of resistance ... Our actors and sculptors and painters and writers and poets must be made to know that we appreciate them, that it is in fact their work that puts starch in our backbones.

Maya Angelou, 1998

various minorities since they are not – is not helpful. It implies that so-called minorities have more in common with each other than they do with people in the so-called majority and that differences of ethnicity and appearance are more fundamental than differences of class, occupation, region, religion and gender. The Commission on the Future of Multi-Ethnic Britain argued in its 2000 report that Britain is more appropriately pictured as a community of citizens and communities.

The reference, first and foremost, is to relationships between the UK's four constituent nations. But also each nation is a community of communities, not a monolithic whole. Each contains many identities and affiliations; each is in a process of development; each has its own internal tensions, arguments and

Views and voices – 26

The nationality called runners

I knew I belonged to millions of other 'Brits' when I stood amongst 15,000 runners in the 10K London Run last July. They, like me, got up early on a rainy Sunday morning, changed quickly in St James's Park, slightly worried about how they looked in their shorts and with a corner of their eye studying the latest piece of gear on other runners. I felt I belonged because I understood the feeling of getting the cheers from hundreds of people along Whitehall and the joy of crossing the finishing line at the Embankment, knowing that you have just run your personal best. I know I belong to the nationality called 'runners', because I see it on their faces every time our paths cross during the morning run in my local park. For similar reasons I know I belong to other communities: husbands, community workers, journalists, computer enthusiasts, South Londoners, plum brandy lovers, Discovery Channel fans...

Zafir Behlic, 2003

contradictions; each influences and impacts on, and in turn is influenced by, others. Every community overlaps with several others and every individual, it follows, belongs to several different communities. The idea of Britain as a community of communities is strikingly expressed in *Views and voices 26*, written by someone who came to Britain recently as a refugee from Bosnia.

Schemes of work

QCA schemes of work particularly relevant to the themes discussed in chapter 2 include *Living in a diverse world; Children's rights, human rights; Local democracy for young citizens; In the media – what's the news?; Debating a global issue; How do we deal with conflict?; Skills of democratic participation; School linking; Challenging racism and discrimination; Global issues, local action.*

Classroom examples

Commemoration

Learners plan, present and take part in a commemorative event about 11 September 2001, using resources published by the Muslim Home School Network, based in the United States, www.muslimhomeschool.com.

We are Britain

Learners study and perform the poems in *We Are Britain* by Benjamin Zephaniah and write similar poems about themselves, illustrated by photographs similar in style to the ones in Zephaniah's book.

Media analysis

Learners study differing accounts of the same event, for example the differences between a report on the website of BBC News and reports in various tabloids. In their analysis they use the questions suggested in *Citizenship and Muslim Perspectives* by Muhammad Imran and Elaine Miskell: What is fact and what is fiction? What language is used? Is there an attempt to present a balanced argument? Are ideas presented as clear-cut, or can you see that even people directly involved are uncertain? Whose voice do you hear through the report? Does the report tell you what to think, or are you presented with evidence so that you can make up your own mind? Who is the target audience?

Please note: There are several further examples of citizenship education in the section on PSHE, pages 42-43.

Design and technology

Overview

Design and technology is relevant to the principles and concepts outlined in chapter 2 in two main ways.

■ Skills and concepts are frequently illustrated with problems and tasks from the real world. Whenever this happens there is an opportunity to reflect issues of personal and cultural identity, shared humanity, difference and diversity, the interdependence of local and global, and conflict and justice

■ Designing and working in three dimensions is a crucial feature of human life in all cultures, countries and traditions, for there are universal human needs for shelter, transport, food preparation and sustainable development. The subject therefore provides a wealth of opportunities for challenging the default position (see page 14) that science and technology belong distinctively to the West.

In addition, design and technology involves skills of analysis, problem-solving, self-evaluation and logical thought that are transferable to discussions of social, moral and political issues. The potential of the subject is well evoked in *Views and voices 27*, taken from the writings of one of the principal pioneers and leaders in the design and technology field of the last 50 years.

Commentary

A recurring requirement at all key stages in the national curriculum is that learners should reflect on their own work and should devise ways of improving it. They are expected to:

■ talk about their own work and that of other people and describe how a product works

■ recognise what they have done well as their work progresses, and suggest things they could do better in the future

■ test and evaluate their products, showing that they understand the situations in which their designs will have to function and are aware of resources as a constraint

■ evaluate how effectively they have used information sources

---

Views and voices – 27

Ever more compelling

The range of work is vast; the history of many Design and Technology activities is as old as humanity itself. Yet only recently have we begun to realise the full potential of this area of the school curriculum.

Not only have we discovered a wide range of new and previously unused processes and materials, but we have also rediscovered the intellectual as well as the practical learning that can take place in work with materials.

Above all we have realised more fundamentally than ever before that, in a modern society, human capacity to use and to modify the environment is critically determined by capacity to understand, plan and utilise resources of three-dimensional materials. Their availability and well-designed manipulation are as essential to the activities of an advanced industrial economy as they have been to those of any previous social system.

... And as the scarcity of natural resources intensifies and the cost of materials produced from them rises, the argument for work in the school that enhances thought and discrimination in their use becomes ever more compelling.

John Eggleston, 2001

Views and voices – 28

Damn fools

The biographer of William Morris (1834-96), imagines his reactions to aspects of modern society

Electronic addiction? Drug culture? Inner city planning? Bottom line banking? Political correctness? Post modernist architecture? Theme parks? Niche retailing? Bargain breaks? Time-share homes? Spaghetti junctions? Shopping malls? Leisure centres? Tele-cottages? Health farms? Saturation advertising? Freebie magazines? Junk mail? Fast food? Course modules? Heritage trails? Craft fayres? Business parks? Garden centres? Sound bites? Opinion polls? Chat shows? Designer clothes? Executive phones? Pulp literature? Video porn? Corporate sponsorship? Market orientated society?...

'Damn'd pigs! Damn'd fools!' You can hear Morris expostulate, robust, fidgety, tremendous, pulling out the hairs (singly) from his great prophetic beard.

Fiona MacCarthy, *William Morris*, 1994

Review and development

On page 54, ten features of good practice in design and technology are listed in order to guide reviews of current provision and to assist with planning future developments.

■ establish a broad range of criteria for evaluating their products, clearly relating their findings to the purpose for which the products were designed and the appropriate use of resources.

Evaluative judgements about their own design and making activities (DMAs), as sketched above, can lead naturally into consideration of design issues in modern urban life and to engagement with the outlook evoked in *Views and voices 28*.

Schemes of work

At key stages 1 and 2, national schemes of work that can be adapted to engage with the themes discussed in chapter 2 include *Homes; Puppets; Storybooks; Photograph frames; Musical instruments; Shelters*. At KS 3 and 4 all assignments, activities and projects concerned with food-resistant materials, textiles, control, professional designers and markets can reflect and be informed by the perspectives in chapter 2.

Classroom examples

Puppets

Learners examine with care, curiosity and respect stick puppets from India, Indonesia and Thailand, and design, make and use their own. Instead or as well, they design and make shadow puppets and theatres.

Playground

Learners devise and administer a questionnaire about fellow-learners' likes and dislikes about the school playground and other public spaces. They propose improvements that could be made and make models or plans to illustrate their proposals.

Buffet meal

Learners design and make an informal buffet for a group of people from a range of religious and cultural backgrounds. They need therefore to research the various cultures to establish probable likes and dislikes.

Storage and packaging

Learners look at ways in which different cultures have stored and preserved food in the past, and at the diversity of methods that still persists. They design and make new containers for use in different parts of the world.

Learners examine samples of packaging in local shops. What appear to be effective methods of marketing, and what are the key points to bear in mind with regard to hygiene and preservation? Learners design and make their own packaging for real or imaginary products.

Clothing

Learners create a display of clothing from different parts of the world and provide labels explaining the technology used to manufacture them from raw material to finished product. As appropriate, they comment also on religious and cultural factors.

Intermediate technology

Learners visit the websites of voluntary organisations concerned with promoting intermediate and appropriate technology, and design and create web pages to summarise their views.

Learners design and make a folding structure capable of supporting material for a temporary shelter at a time of a natural or humanitarian disaster, either in the UK or elsewhere.

Sustainable development

Taking ideas from the pack *Live well, live wisely* published by the Intermediate Technology Development Group, learners study the concept of sustainability throughout the world; research recycling and waste collection activities in their own locality; and compare and contrast projects in their local neighbourhood with projects elsewhere. They then design and model a waste collection point that could be set up in their own school, and an awareness-raising and publicity campaign to encourage other learners – and all staff – to use it.

As part of the project they evaluate various products in use at their school, considering questions such as the following. What raw materials were used to make the product? How and where were the raw materials extracted and processed? How was the product manufactured? How was it transported to a market? How is it advertised? How is it reused or disposed of after its first use? How is the packaging reused or disposed of?

English

Overview

Literacy has two aspects:

- development of skills of communication and expression, both orally and in writing

- study and appreciation of stories, poetry, drama and non-fiction by others.

The subject is therefore relevant to the themes outlined in chapter 2 when:

- in their own writing and speaking learners have opportunities to explore issues of personal and cultural identity, shared humanity, difference, diversity, conflict and justice

- in the study and appreciation of literature written by others, attention is drawn as appropriate to the ways writers have handled issues of personal and cultural identity, shared humanity, difference, diversity, racism, conflict and justice

- literature by others is selected from a wide range of literary traditions and shows ways in which writers in different circumstances influence and inspire each other.

In addition, skills of deliberation, narrative and advocacy, both in writing and in various kinds of oral situation, are fundamental in citizenship education and PSHE.

Views and voices – 29

Never die

It is my wish that the voice of the storyteller will never die in Africa, that all the children in Africa may experience the wonder of books, and that they will never lose the capacity to enlarge their earthly dwelling place with the magic of stories.

Nelson Mandela, 2002

Commentary

The three attainment targets of speaking and listening, reading and writing all have to be developed in relation to specific subject-matter. In English, as in art and design (see page 22) the subject-matter can be summarised as *social, cultural and environmental issues* and *the learners themselves and their experiences*.

Views and voices – 30

The desire to know

I hadn't realised I was so *ignorant*, Celie. The little I knew about my own self wouldn't have filled a thimble! And to think Miss Beasley always said I was the smartest child she ever taught! But one thing I do thank her for, for teaching me to learn for myself, by reading and studying and writing a clear hand. And for keeping alive in me the desire to know.

Alice Walker, *The Color Purple*, 1983

The skills that learners develop in English are directly bound up with qualities of self-awareness and self-confidence, with respect and attention towards the views of others and with what the young person quoted in *Views and voices 30* calls 'the desire to know'. Learners are expected to develop:

- increasing confidence and competence in using standard English as appropriate and making appropriate choices of language in formal situations

- sensitivity to the tone, undertone and other indications of speakers' intentions

- increasing confidence in understanding texts that are challenging in terms of length, complexity of language and sophistication of ideas

- language and actions in drama to explore and convey situations, characters and emotions.

Such learning can naturally promote reflection and understanding of the contested meanings of the term ethnicity, as recalled in *Views and voices 31*, and consideration of so-called political correctness.

Views and voices – 31

Groucho Club

At the launch in London's Groucho Club last month of Meera Syal's second novel, *Life Isn't All Ha Ha Hee Hee,* the chairman of her publishers, Transworld, described her writing as being about 'ethnic life'. Is it only black people who have ethnicity? One wonders if he would imagine his own existence, at the Groucho Club, the golf course or the boardroom, to be part of some 'ethnic life'.

Maya Jaggi, 1999

Review and development

On page 55, ten features of good practice in English are listed in order to guide reviews of current provision and to assist with planning future developments.

Views and voices – 32

How we survive

Where are we? This whole Asians Are Groovy thing amuses me but I don't trust it. None of us want to be remembered merely as this year's flavour, to be discarded when the next cute ethnic phase comes along. Having exposure is fine and dandy, being feted and noticed is important, but it's how we survive from here that counts.

... Around me I hear teenagers mixing cockney glottals with black patois and Punjabi slang. It's a new language with a unique beat and it drums through all our work, the new Londoners. Innit?

Meera Syal, 2003

Messages from EAL

Specialists in teaching English as an additional language have developed substantial expertise that is relevant to all learners, not to bilingual learners only. They draw a fundamental distinction between interpersonal conversational skills on the one hand and academic language skills on the other. It is the latter that is required for progress and success in the national curriculum.

All learners benefit in a classroom where there is a lively interest in synonyms and nuances of meaning, in the origins and derivations of words, and in the nature and uses of metaphor. All benefit from activities which:

- use visual material, particularly material that communicates key concepts

- involve sorting, matching and reasoning

- involve practical and manipulative activities

- are cognitively demanding and challenging even though the language for them may be reduced in length or grammatical complexity

- require genuine communication and exploratory talk

Schemes of work

QCA schemes of work particularly relevant to the ideas discussed in chapter 2 include *Poetry and stories with familiar, predictable structures and patterned language from a range of cultures; Information texts including non-chronological*

reports; oral and performance poetry from different cultures; Letters written for a range of purposes, to recount, explain, enquire, congratulate, complain; Persuasive writing, adverts, flyers; Autobiography and biography, diaries and journals; standard English and dialect; comparing languages; bias and objectivity; implied and explicit meanings; 'infotainment'.

Classroom examples

Journey stories
Using a resource such as *The Journey* by Marcia Hutchinson (details in bibliography) learners conduct interviews with people who took part in a major journey (from another country to UK, or from one part of UK to another) in their youth and construct pieces of prose which tell their stories. They include expectations before the journey began; things that happened on the way; initial feelings on arrival; and tasks of settling down and developing a sense of belonging.

Race and diversity
Using the collections from Badger Publishing entitled *Celebrating Difference: positive images of race for infants* and *Challenging Racism through Literature: positive images of race for juniors*, learners write reviews and give talks; write to the authors; and take part in a mini literature festival at which awards are made to the books considered best.

Identity and struggle
Learners read and study the stories for teenagers in *Walking a Tightrope* edited by Rehana Ahmed and comment in various genres of writing, and in various oral styles, on character, setting and mood; author perspective and voice; significant detail; starting and finishing; and creativity in language and narrative. They then write similar stories themselves.

Shadows
Learners use the ideas, principles, techniques and practical instructions in *Let the Shadows Speak* by Franzeska Ewart to present traditional folktales and to engage the audience in discussion and argument about matters of current importance in the school.

Please note: Many of the activities outlined in other sections of this chapter are relevant to English. See in particular citizenship and PSHE.

Geography

Overview

Geography is relevant to the principles and concepts discussed in chapter 2 when learners:

- are helped to know better their immediate environment and neighbourhood and to see their locality within the wider context of regional, national and international affairs

- study constants and universals in relationships between human beings and their physical environment

- develop understanding of concepts such as globalisation, world society, interdependence, sustainable development and spaceship earth

- reflect on ways in which personal, cultural and national identity is bound up with perceptions of, and feelings about, natural landscape and public spaces.

Views and voices – 33
Did not even know

Geography had been one of his strong points. He was aware of the rivers of Asia in their order, and of the principal products of Uruguay; and he could name the capitals of nearly all the United States.

But he had not been instructed for five minutes in the geography of his native country, of which he knew neither the boundaries nor the rivers nor the terrene characteristics. He could have drawn a map of the Orinoco, but he could not have found the Trent in a day's march; he did not even know where his drinking water came from.

Clayhanger by Arnold Bennett, set in 1872

Commentary

From the earliest stages of the national curriculum, learners are expected to develop skills in describing where things are in the simple contexts of the classroom, school grounds and local area, and to be aware of the wider world. Later, study of geography involves:

- identifying and describing examples of the ways people affect their physical environment and of projects to manage such interactions

- recognising ways in which change may damage or improve environments

Views and voices – 34
Exhilarating

One thing is certain: the wider world, the school system and the teaching of geography will not stay the same for very long. Teachers have been saying for some time now that schools must educate pupils for a life of continual change. It is salutary to be reminded that we are part of the world, and will ourselves be inevitably involved in these changes in an uncertain future. There is perhaps some consolation in the fact that while excessive change can be uncomfortable and exhausting, the years since 1960 have shown that, with a minimum of luck and a willingness to adapt, it can be both exhilarating and rewarding.

Rex Beddis, 1983

Views and voices – 35
The landscape of our country

Tonight, in the quiet of this room, I find that what really remains with me from this first day's travel is not Salisbury Cathedral, nor any of the other charming sights of this city, but rather that marvellous view encountered this morning of the rolling English countryside. Now I am quite prepared to believe that other countries can offer more obviously spectacular scenery. Indeed, I have seen in encyclopaedia and the *National Geographic Magazine* breathtaking photographs of sights from various corners of the globe; magnificent canyons and waterfalls, raggedly beautiful mountains. It has never, of course, been my privilege to have seen such things at first hand, but I will nevertheless hazard this with some confidence: the English landscape at its finest – such as I saw it this morning – possesses a quality that the landscape of other nations, however more superficially dramatic, inevitably fail to possess. It is, I believe, a quality that will mark out the English landscape to any objective observer as the most deeply satisfying in the world, and this quality is probably best summed up by the term 'greatness'... We call this land of ours Great Britain, and there may be those who believe this a somewhat immodest practice. Yet I would venture that the landscape of our country alone would justify the use of this lofty adjective.

Remains of the Day by Kazuo Ishiguro, set in 1956

■ drawing out similarities and differences between places and recognising the ways in which places are interdependent.

With regard to skills, learners are expected to:

■ demonstrate independence in identifying appropriate questions and issues

■ appreciate the significance of attitudes and values, including their own

■ provide coherent arguments and substantiated conclusions

■ critically evaluate sources of evidence.

Such skills and activities may provoke the kinds of reflection on national identity and sense of personal belonging that are shown in *Views and voices 35*. The reflection is not strictly speaking geographical. But it starts explicitly from a popular understanding of the nature of geography and is a reminder that the study of geography inevitably involves feelings and values.

Schemes of work

At KS1 and 2, QCA schemes of work particularly relevant to the ideas discussed in chapter 2 include *Around our school – the local area; An island home; A village in India; What's in the news; Global eye; Connecting ourselves to the world; A contrasting locality overseas; How can we improve the area we can see from our window?; Passport to the world.*

At KS3 relevant schemes of work include *Making connections; People everywhere; Exploring England; Shopping – past, present and future; Images of a country; Can the earth cope – ecosytems, population and resources; The global fashion industry; Comparing countries; Local action, global effects.*

Classroom examples

Guided walk of local neighbourhood
Using *Global Reading,* published by Reading International Solidarity Centre (details and a quiz at www.risc.org.uk/introgame.html) learners consider their immediate neighbourhood and ask: Where does this road lead to? Where did the stone for this building come from? How did the person who built this house make their money? Why is this street named after a place in India? Where do goods come from in the shops? After further research, some of it including the use of digital photography, they add information on outline maps of the area and produce a world map display, highlighting the places to which their area is linked. They build up their local-global map, adding appropriate symbols and a key. They then develop a guided walk with activities at each stage to introduce the variety of ways in which the area is linked to the rest of the world.

Globalisation
Learners consider five quotations from various recent reports, lectures and speeches: the UK minister for international development, world reports on The Gambia and Mongolia, a group of Caribbean ministers; and Vandana Shiva's *Respect for the Earth.* They list ten statements or claims about globalisation and rank them in the order in which they agree with them. They then consider the implications for an issue currently being debated in their own locality. (The texts of the quotations mentioned above, together with many other useful discussion materials, are in *Globalisation – what's it all about?* published by the Tide Centre, Birmingham.)

Land
Learners are given a set of photographs and sort them according to whether they illustrate the concept of 'land'. They then construct a definition of the concept and compare it with the definition in the Collins English Dictionary. This activity is followed by one entitled 'Who said that?' They are shown photographs of a local park established ten years ago and given quotations from seven people about it – a park attendant, a teenage girl, a mother with young children, the architect, a nine year old, a local councillor and an office worker. These activities lead into studies of land use in various countries; discussion of preferred futures for the world and the local neighbourhood; and a simulated parliamentary or council debate. (For full information see *Your Place or Mine?* by Maggie Lunan and Susan McIntosh.)

History

Overview

History is relevant to the principles and concepts discussed in chapter 2 when learners:

- study the history of their own local neighbourhood and see it within wider regional, national and international contexts

- see similarities and commonalities in societies at different periods, particularly with regard to the management of conflict and change and campaigns and measures to create and maintain justice

- become familiar with the impact on Britain of events and developments overseas, and the impact of events in Britain on other countries and places

- reflect on the changing nature of British identity over the centuries

- become increasingly aware that human beings have differing perceptions of, and develop differing narratives about, the same events.

- become familiar with different and conflicting interpretations and narratives of the same event or series of events

- be aware of ethnic, cultural, regional and religious diversity, and differences of social class and gender, in Britain over the centuries as also in other societies.

A constant requirement in history is that learners should have a questioning attitude towards the narratives and interpretations that they encounter. They:

- use and sift through a range of sources, including interviews, documents, speeches, eye-witness accounts, recordings, CD ROMS, databases, websites, pictures and photographs, music and artefacts, and visits to historic buildings museums, galleries and sites

- identify and evaluate sources of information and use them critically to reach and support conclusions

---

Views and voices – 36

So they make sense

We scurry about like ants with a stick poked into their ant-heap. Why the sticks have been poked, we don't know, but our lives and houses are upside-down just the same. That's what war means: blunders and muddle, and doing things without understanding why you're doing them. A long time later, if you're lucky, someone comes along and writes things down so that they make sense, and calls his story history.

Helen Dunmore, *The Siege*, 2001

Commentary

There is a recurring requirement in the national curriculum that learners should know the history of their own area, and that general concepts of change, cause and influence should be illustrated with local examples.

Learners are required to be familiar with similarities and commonalities between different historical periods. Also, however, they are required to recognise and study differences, including differences between their own lives and the lives of people in the past. Further, they are required to:

Views and voices – 37

History so physically present

At Lime Street Station I sit and wait for my train. As the minutes tick by, I watch the pigeons circling high in the roof of the station. The world's first railway service was inaugurated in Liverpool, but what a farce. As the train moved off, it ran over and killed the Liverpool MP who had been officially observing. A history hitched to tragedy.

A train pulls in and I can hear the uncivilised braying of football fans readying themselves for a Saturday afternoon of revelry. I am glad I am leaving. It is disquieting to be in a place where history is so physically present, yet so glaringly absent from people's consciousness.

But where is it any different? Maybe this is the modern condition, and Liverpool is merely acting out this reality with an honest vigour. If so, this dissonance between the two states seems to have engendered both a cynical wit and a clinical depression in the souls of Liverpool's citizens.

As I sidestep my way around the fat-bellied football fans and move to catch my train. I silently wish everybody a happy Christmas.

The Atlantic Sound by Caryl Phillips, 2000

- analyse and explain why there are different historical interpretations of events, people and changes

- select, organise and deploy relevant information to produce structured work, making appropriate use of dates and terms.

Schemes of work

At KS1 and KS2, QCA schemes of work particularly relevant to the themes in chapter 2 include *Why have people invaded and settled in Britain in the past?*; *How did life change ion our locality in Victorian times?*; *How has life in Britain changed in Britain since 1948*; *and How can we find out about the Indus Valley civilisation?*

At KS3, particularly relevant schemes of work include What were the achievements of Islamic states 600-1600; Moghul India and the coming of the British 1526-1857; The British Empire – how did Britain control a quarter of the world by 1900; How and why did the Holocaust happen?; and Black peoples of America – from slavery to equality. Further schemes of work centrally concerned with issues of conflict and justice include Industrial changes – action and reaction; The Franchise – why did it take so long for women to get the vote; and Divided Ireland – why is peace so hard to achieve?

Classroom examples

'We also served'

Learners use the pack developed by Birmingham Advisory and Support Service on the significant contributions made by service men and women from South Asia, Africa and the Caribbean to the British forces in the 1914-1918 and 1939-1945 world wars. Entitled *We Also Served*, the pack contains sixteen fascinating accounts of people who volunteered to fight in the trenches, to fly fighter planes and bombers, to work as seamen, and to serve in field hospitals. The pack is intended for key stages two and three but can be used also with older and younger learners.

Local neighbourhood and community

Learners study ways in which their local area has changed over the course of time. They investigate education, houses and housing, migration and movement to the area from overseas and other parts of the UK; the building of factories; markets; religious observance; treatment of the poor and care of the sick; law and order; sport, leisure and the impact of national and international events and developments.

Hot seat

Learners interrogate a teacher or other adult who takes the role of an Elizabethan buccaneer such as Sir John Hawkins. What is his view of the world? How does he try to justify his actions and exploits? How able is he to imagine the feelings, views and experiences of people to whom he caused suffering? What is his reaction to the writings of Olaudah Equiano, and those of other abolitionists?

Civilisations and stories

In groups or as individuals learners study cultures and narratives such as the following, and report on similarities and differences with regard to issues of equality, resolution of conflict, and justice and fairness between the sexes and between ethnic groups: Islamic civilisations, including Muhammad and Makkah and the empires of Islam in Africa; Imperial China from the First Emperor to Kublai Khan; India from the Mughal Empire to the coming of the British; the civilisations of Peru; indigenous peoples of North America; African-American people in the Americas and the African diaspora in the UK; West African empires; the Sikhs and the Mahrattas.

National identity

Learners create and illustrate time-lines showing relationships over the centuries between England, Ireland, Scotland and Wales, noting different perspectives and stories in the four nations at different times, and in different social classes, and the impact of urbanisation and the Empire. They investigate current views of British identity and of how it is changing.

Information and communications technology

Overview

ICT is relevant to the principles and concepts discussed in chapter 2 when:

- tasks, assignments and practical projects reflect the multi-ethnic nature of modern Britain, and touch on issues of shared humanity, global interdependence, racism, conflict and justice

- websites and software reflect experience in a wide range of countries, cultures and communities

- there is increasing awareness that computers and the internet are part of everyday life for billions of people throughout the world, but awareness also that access to computers is unequally distributed.

Further, ICT can be an essential and invaluable feature of school-linking schemes. The skill of coping with potential overloads of information, and therefore of evaluating, sifting and selecting, are transferable to all other subjects and to all the topics discussed in chapter 2.

Commentary

When working with ICT, learners are expected by national curriculum requirements to:

- interpret and question the plausibility of information and recognise that poor quality information leads to unreliable results

- find and interrogate information, understanding the need for care in framing questions

- amend and combine different forms of information from a variety of sources

- generate and amend work

- refine the quality of their presentations showing an awareness of the intended audience

- compare their use of ICT with other methods

- select the information they need for different purposes, check its accuracy and organise it in a form suitable for processing.

- structure and refine information in different forms and styles for specific purposes and audiences

- explore the effects of changing the variables in an ICT-based model

- monitor and measure external events with sensors

- assess the use of ICT in their work and reflect critically in order to make improvements in subsequent work.

Such activities require a critical disposition and capacity to analyse, and awareness of the internet's limitations. The dangers of information overload and unrealistic expectations are alluded to in *Views and voices 39*.

Views and voices – 38

More and more powerful

Computer chips are getting smaller and smaller and more and more powerful all the time. They're improving faster than any other machine in history. It's been calculated that if cars had developed at the same rate as computers over the last thirty years you'd be able to buy a Rolls Royce today for under a pound, and it would do three million miles to the gallon.

David Lodge, *Thinks*, 2001

Views and voices – 39

All for the price of a local call

Suddenly the Internet is the solution to everything. The Prime Minister is lying awake at night trying to think of a way forward for the peace process in Northern Ireland. 'Have you thought about looking on the Internet?' asks Cherie. And obviously there it is, instantly available and all for the price of a local call. The way to end world poverty, the secret of eternal happiness, the cure for cancer – apparently you can find out anything from the internet. The only problem is that when you enter the words 'cure' and 'cancer', your search engine will find four million sites, the first of which is the diary of a fifteen-year-old boy from Milwaukee whose favourite band is the Cure and whose star sign is Cancer. And for some reason you find yourself reading ten pages about his trip to summer camp in Vermont before you accept that this site isn't going to have the information you were looking for.

John O'Farrell, 2000

Review and development

On page 58, ten features of good practice in ICT are listed in order to guide reviews of current provision and to assist with planning further development.

Schemes of work

The national schemes of work are entirely concerned with ICT skills. They can therefore be used with any subject matter in order to access, select and interpret information; recognise patterns, relationships and behaviours; model, predict and hypothesise; test reliability and accuracy; review and modify work to improve its quality; present information; communicate with others; improve efficiency; and develop qualities of creativity, risk-taking, confidence and independence. At KS3 relevant schemes of work include *Public information systems; Information – reliability, validity and bias; and Global communication – negotiating and managing data.*

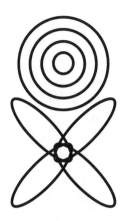

Classroom examples

Ectastic

Learners visit the Ectastic site of Hagbourne Primary School, Oxfordshire (www.hagbourne.oxon.sch.uk/ecotastic) – 'we created this website,' they are told, 'to help other schools and people at home to be more eco friendly. We want to share all our eco experiences with others, so the world will be a much happier place for us all to live in...' They note that the school recently won a major award in the international Childnet Academy scheme (www.childnetacademy.org), so they visit the sites of other winners throughout the world and decide which they consider best.

Tourism

In geography, learners look at tourism within the local community and identify emerging patterns. This enables them to extend their analysis of local situations within national contexts and to recognise global patterns. They analyse brochures, and holiday programmes on television, and in four different groups they use ICT, including an internet message board, to research negative and positive effects in four locations, the Alps, the Caribbean, India and Ghana. Using presentation software they discuss sustainable development and make reasoned geographical arguments. The presentations raise questions about form as well as content, for example the use of humour, maps, photographs and keywords.

Evaluation of websites

Learners evaluate a range of websites about race and diversity issues, considering features of style, navigation and content. They use this information to plan and design their own website about racial justice and cultural diversity for a particular audience. They produce a project plan, breaking down work into a series of smaller tasks. In their work they consider efficiency, fitness for purpose and audience needs. For example, they might use ICT to convert and compress graphic files to allow faster download times. They make informed use of automated features in software to create a navigational menu on each page. Where appropriate, they integrate applications. For example, they may include a response form on their site, to collect information from users. They test and refine their site using the school intranet.

Visits to museums and exhibitions

Learners plan a real or imaginary day trip to a museum specialising in issues of cultural diversity and equality, for example the Museum of the British Empire and Commonwealth at Bristol. They use the internet and paper-based materials to find out the entry fees and use route-finding software to determine the distance. They enter this data into a spreadsheet model prepared in collaboration with the teacher and add data on cost of transport. They use the model to establish the cost per learner. The teacher then provides a number of possible scenarios, for example an increase in the number of learners, and learners explore the model to provide answers. Groups make presentations to the rest of the class about their preferred destinations.

Campaigning for justice

Working in pairs, learners create a web page about a particularly important movement, campaign or personality in the development of racial justice. They need to research the subject and then write a short introduction identifying key facts and concepts, for example, Who? What? When? Where? Why? They also find or create between one and three images that can be scanned in to illustrate their text.

Mathematics

Overview

Mathematics is relevant to the principles and key concepts outlined in chapter 2 in two principal ways:

■ Whenever mathematical concepts and processes are illustrated with regard to 'the real world', and when situations are described and analysed with mathematical symbols, words and diagrams, there are opportunities to engage with issues in local, national and global society

■ Mathematics is a universal human skill, not a body of knowledge which is distinctively western.

In addition, mathematics involves skills of analysis, problem-solving and logical thought that are transferable to discussions of social, moral and political issues.

Commentary

At all key stages there are opportunities to stress that mathematics is a universal human activity and that some of the most important advances in mathematics were made outside Europe.

In mathematics as in all other subjects, learners develop skills of monitoring, assessing and evaluating. They:

■ study data handling through practical activities and are introduced to a quantitative approach to probability

■ learn statistical techniques to analyse data

■ use short chains of deductive reasoning, develop their own proofs, and understand the importance of proof in mathematics

■ draw conclusions of their own, explaining their reasoning

■ give reasons for the choices they make when investigating within mathematics, and explain why particular lines of enquiry or procedure are followed and others rejected.

Schemes of work

The national numeracy strategy lays great stress at all key stages on real-life problems.

Review and development

On page 59, ten features of good practice in mathematics are listed in order to guide reviews of current provision and to assist with planning further development.

One equals one?

It has been a general belief that the teaching of maths is different from the teaching of history or sociology or political science. Such a belief asserts that in the latter subjects there are different points of view, while in maths facts are true irrespective of culture or of the individual or of time. I came to believe that this is a very misleading belief that affects our teaching of maths negatively. 'The First World War took place in the period between 1914 and 1918' is a historical fact, but its description and interpretation differ from one person to another and from one nation to another. Similarly, I believe, 'one equals one' is a mathematical fact, but its description and interpretation and application differ from one situation to another and from one culture to another. A fresh and delicious apple is not equal to a rotten apple. A certain chair is not equal to another chair in all its details no matter how identical they seem to be. No person is equal to himself the next day. One dollar in 1970 is not equal to one dollar in 1980. And so on. Strictly speaking, then, 'one equals one' does not have true instances or applications in the real world.

The truth of the matter is that in schools and in all our teaching we keep the world of reality separate from the world of abstraction. In the world of abstraction, we usually agree about facts. But in the real world we face many interpretations and meanings and ways of looking at these facts; so we argue and we fight. For example, people agree one equals one is true in abstraction, but antagonistic feelings and different opinions emerge when we say for example that women are equal to men or that one vote for Jordan (with two million people) in the UN is equal to one vote for the US (with 200 million people) in the UN. Teaching with meanings and by relating the abstract world to the real world makes maths more relevant and more useful.

In addition, it helps students appreciate remarks such as Einstein's often cited remark, 'As far as the laws of maths refer to reality, they are not certain; and as far as they are certain, they do not refer to reality'.

Munir Fasheh, 1980

Classroom Examples

Counting
Learners commit to memory the rhymes and poems in *A Caribbean Counting Book* by Faustin Charles, published by Barefoot Books, and act them out in a range of ways. They compare them with rhymes they already know and discuss aspects of the vocabulary and non-mathematical content.

Global village
Learners work with the picture book *If the World were a Village* by David Smith (details in bibliography) and present the same statistical data in alternative forms. The topics include nationalities, languages, ages, religions, air and water, schooling and literacy, money and possessions, electricity, food, and past and present. There are many classroom activities suggested at acblack.com/globalvillage

Identities, belongings and statistics
Learners work with data and materials at the Census at School website, based at Nottingham Trent University (www.censusatschool.ntu.ac.uk). There are questionnaires for them to fill in, downloadable worksheets, an interactive histogram, a poem, a song, factsheets about the 2001 census of population, and a wealth of activities integrating statistical analysis with geography, history, science, ICT and citizenship. There are sister sites in Canada, New Zealand, Queensland and South Australia.

Demography
Learners use data published by the Office of National Statistics relating to the 2001 census of population and construct, on paper and using ICT, a range of graphs and charts and identify which styles of numerical representation are most suitable for various purposes and contexts.

They then present concise, reasoned arguments, using symbols, diagrams, graphs and related explanatory text.

The state of the nation
Working in groups, learners assemble mathematical illustrations of propositions in official reports and design tests which would establish whether the situation is improving or getting worse. For example, they consider statements in the DfES's five-year plan for education, or in *The State of the Nation* by the Institute for Public Policy Research. The latter is downloadable from www.ippr.org.uk. It contains statistics on wealth and income distribution, social mobility, crime and fear of crime, differentials in the pay of women and men, and levels of child poverty in UK and other European countries.

Modern foreign languages

Overview

The study of modern foreign languages is relevant to the concepts and key ideas discussed in chapter 2 when learners:

- understand and appreciate different countries, cultures, people and communities

- appreciate that language is a universal human characteristic, and see similarities as well as differences between their own language and others

- realise that no language is intrinsically 'better' for all purposes than all others

- appreciate 'diversity within diversity', for example the great diversity of class, region and cultural background and tradition for whom French is the first language

- are aware that languages are continually evolving and borrowing from each other.

Views and voices – 43

Curse?

There are people who say it was God's curse to confound the speech of men, but I do not see that. That there are so many different kinds of flower is no curse, so why for many different languages?

Anthony Burgess, *Earthly Powers*, 1980

Views and voices – 44

Sweet melody

We speak in Bengali,
we write in Bengali.

We see the entire world
through its green glow.

We adorn the minarets of our minds
with its countless flowers,
illuminating the sky.

With its light in our hands
we journey across the world.

Through its sweet melody
we learn the languages of others

Rabindranath Tagore
Translated by Anowara Jehaan

Views and voices – 45

Unaware

The speaker of a language is like a swimmer moving effortlessly and at will in water while unaware that he is wet. Speakers of different languages are like swimmers in different ponds.

Andreas Fuglesang, 1982

Commentary

Learning a foreign language has the potential for showing that many countries are linguistically and culturally diverse, and that many languages, including English, French and Spanish, are spoken in more than one country. It can also enhance respect for bilingualism and multilingualism and remind learners that the ability to communicate in two or more languages is widespread throughout the world.

Learners who are themselves bilingual, or whose parents or grandparents are bilingual, should feel that their linguistic skills and insights are valued by the modern foreign languages curriculum, and their experience and specialist knowledge should be drawn on whenever appropriate.

Views and voices – 46

Discovered and rediscovered

Although I lost faith in politics long ago, I still believe in the power of the word, and especially in the power of translation.

The globalisation of capital threatens to extinguish the spirit of each culture, but one positive change has come from this movement. It has shed light on the importance of translation. Translation can, of course, be seen as a tool that facilitates the globalisation of capital and thus contributes to the overall deadening of cultures, but when poetry is translated it works against those effects.

The particularities of one culture, expressed through poetry, can be appreciated by readers of another because of translation. My work on translation from Arabic into English and vice versa has thus been immensely spiritually rewarding. I have discovered and rediscovered many aspects of my own culture.

Saadi Simawe, *Iraqi Poetry Today*, 2003

Textbooks, posters, tapes, videos and ICT materials should:

- reflect the fact that speakers of the target language are not homogeneous in terms of religion, culture, ethnicity and nationality

- help learners to know more about the cultural, social and historical contexts in which the target language had developed and is now used

- be concerned with issues of identity and relationships, and with social, moral and political issues, that are intrinsically interesting and connect with learners' own lives and concerns

- show that the ability to communicate with speakers of other languages can nurture mutual respect, tolerance and understanding

- help learners to appreciate features of their own linguistic identity

- help learners to move away from an anglocentric or ethnocentric perspective, and to see themselves as world citizens

- develop respect for the skills of translators and interpreters.

Schemes of work

The schemes of work for modern foreign languages are to do with grammatical structures and with the communicative use of the target language in various common settings. The schemes provide plenty of opportunities for exploring issues of personal, cultural and linguistic identity and issues in cross-cultural communication.

Classroom examples

Interpreting course

Learners with oral fluency in a language other than English are given training to develop their skills so that they can act as interpreters at parents evenings. This involves agreement on whether and how to translate specialist terms and ethical issues around impartiality and confidentiality. The course forms part of the school's curriculum enrichment programme and is linked with a university-run scheme. It leads to a certificate recognised by UCAS and can therefore help students to gain a university place.

The nature of language

Working in groups, learners research key features of various languages, each group taking a different language. Examples include not only modern foreign languages spoken by the learners themselves but also American Sign Language, British Sign Language, Lingua Franca and Middle English, and visual languages such as Media Glyphs. They use www.ilovelanguages.com as their starting point and collect information also through the websites of the Refugee Council and Portsmouth Ethnic Minority Achievement Service.

Induction course

An induction course in modern foreign languages is taught in the first term of year 7. All pupils learn French and German and either Panjabi or Urdu, each for ten hours, before choosing one of these as their main foreign language for key stage 3. There is an emphasis on transferable language-learning skills and on awareness of the way in which languages work.

Learners explore the relationships between different languages, including links between South Asian and European languages, and the cultural and social contexts in which language is used.

Visit

Learners go on an imaginary trip to a Francophone country. Introduce the idea of an imaginary visit, for example *Nous allons visiter la Suisse/La Martinique/le Canada/la Côte d'Ivoire. C'est une bonne idée? Qui a un passeport?* Real timetables are used, to revise telling the time, and there is talk about how long it takes to get to a place. Each learner makes their own 'passport' with relevant details and writes a personal biography based on the book *L'Histoire de Ma Vie* by Ulfet Mahmout and Alan Thompson, published by Mantra Books.

In an imaginary airport waiting room the flight is announced (*Air France annonce le vol 345 à destination Montréal. Les passagers sont priés de se rendre à la porte numéro 6*) and once inside the 'aircraft' the teacher takes the role of flight attendant and acts out simplified safety precautions. (*Pour attacher la ceinture de sécurité, faites comme ceci. En cas d'urgence le masque à oxygène descendra. Mettez le masque sur la bouche et respirez normalement. Le gilet de sauvetage est sous le siège. Le capitaine et son équipage vous souhaitent un bon voyage.*)

Scrapbooks and diaries are compiled about the trip, in English as well as in French.

Please note: some of the examples outlined above are adapted from material on the QCA *Respect for All* website.

Music

Overview

Music has two aspects:

- development of skills of performance
- study and appreciation of work by others.

The subject is therefore relevant to the big ideas and key concepts outlined in the previous chapter in the following three ways:

- In their own expressive work learners can be given opportunities to explore issues of personal and cultural identity, shared humanity, difference, diversity, conflict and justice
- In the study and appreciation of music created by others, attention can be drawn as appropriate to the ways composers have handled issues of personal and cultural identity, shared humanity, difference, diversity, conflict and justice
- The music created by others can be selected from a wide range of cultural and artistic traditions and can show ways in which composers in different traditions influence and inspire each other.

Commentary

The making of music by individuals and communities is a universal human characteristic. There are common elements in musical traditions, including compositional techniques, devices, resources, cultural and historical contexts, genres, conventions and processes, and there are common

> ### Views and voices – 47
>
> ## I want to be part
>
> Into my mind comes an extraordinarily beautiful sound. I am nine years old. I am sitting between Mr and Mrs Formby in a state of anticipation. On the seats all around us are people chattering and rustling programmes. Into the circus ring enter not elephants and lions but a group of men and women, many of them bearing amazing instruments, gleaming and glowing. A small, frail man enters to applause such as I have never heard before, followed by the strange, absolute silence of a multitude.
>
> He brings down a stick and a huge and lovely noise fills the world. More than anything else I want to be part of such a noise.
>
> Vikram Seth, *Silent Music*

> ### Views and voices – 48
>
> ## Reverence
>
> ... I always want to write erotic music. I want to write sensual/sensuous music. Not only about love between men and women, but in a much more universal sense about the sensuality of the mechanism of the universe, about life...
>
> ... I suddenly imagined 100 years of time flowing through this man-made space, so full of special meaning, called Carnegie Hall. It was if I could hear the Hall murmuring from the numberless cracks between the layers of those years...
>
> Although I am basically self-taught – I consider Debussy my teacher – the most important elements are colour, light and shadow. I feel a deep reverence for the precise workings and the great order in nature, and still wish to learn more from nature as I compose music.
>
> Toru Takemitsu, quoted in concert programme notes, 1998

human concerns, aspirations and strivings. Each tradition, however, combines the common ingredients in its own way.

There has frequently been interaction between different musical traditions in both classical and popular music. In more recent years many composers and performers have increasingly seen themselves as members of a single world community of musicians and freely choose to be influenced by each other. In schools, it is often valuable and relevant to start programmes of work with aspects of contemporary world music, and other examples of fusion and cross-fertilisation.

Learners need to hear unfamiliar music as well as familiar, and are often receptive to new sounds, explorations and experiences. The teaching of music can foster attitudes of openness and curiosity; appreciation and celebration of difference; and keenness to learn from others.

For many learners, music is a powerful expression and reflection of the various communities to which belong. It therefore has the potential to help them:

- improve self-confidence
- recognise how and why they respond differently to different kinds of music – classical, popular, jazz, world, and various kinds of fusion

Review and development

On page 61, ten features of good practice in music are listed in order to guide reviews of current provision and to assist with planning further development.

Views and voices – 49

Images from the imagination

My true function ... is to continue an age-old tradition, fundamental to our civilisation, which goes back into pre-history and will go forward into the unknown future. This tradition is to create images from the depths of the imagination and give them form ... For it is only through images that the inner world communicates at all. Images of the past, shapes of the future. Images of vigour for a decadent period, images of calm for one too violent. Images of reconciliation for worlds torn by division. And in an age of mediocrity and shattered dreams, images of abounding, generous, exuberant beauty.

Michael Tippett, *Moving into Aquarius*, 1964

- make comparisons between familiar and unfamiliar

- participate in wider groupings, and collaborate and cooperate

- develop empathy and respect for people different from themselves, and for identities, communities and traditions with which they are unfamiliar

- give and receive feedback and praise

- challenge stereotypes, bullying and aggressive behaviour.

Music is often used to express feelings not only in personal life (joy, sadness, grief, love, longing, serenity) but also in social and public life – including war and shared tragedy, loyalty and patriotism, and times of collective rejoicing.

The points mentioned above should be reflected in posters and illustrations around the school; in the range of instruments available for use in class; at school assemblies; and in the repertoire and performance groups at school concerts.

Schemes of work

The national schemes of work for music are to do with skills, genres, instruments and sound, not content. They can therefore be used, if schools wish, with the themes outlined in chapter 2.

Classroom examples

Aspects of fusion

Learners compose a piece that integrates different styles of music representing cultural heritages in the school. The music on which they draw includes Pachelbel's *Canon*, rock, jazz, reggae and tabla and dhol. The piece is performed in an assembly for Year 7 learners entitled *Our School*.

Learners visit their local city centre armed with minidisk recorders and record a wide range of city music – buskers, a gospel choir, a steel band – and create a collage for presentation to others.

The pentatonic scale

Learners sing the notes of the Japanese *In* scale, a minor pentatonic scale, and compare it with the major scale used in traditional music in the British Isles. They perform the Japanese song *Sakura* and *Bonnie Banks of Loch Lomond* and compare the effects of the scales, the word setting and the melodic shapes. They listen to a recording of *Sakura* for koto and shamsin and note the use of 'fills' using the notes of the *In* scale.

They then improvise their own class performance of *Sakura* using a pitched instrument such a xylophone. Finally, they compose their own songs to the words of haiku verses written by themselves, using the notes of the *In* scale and incorporating a pitched instrumental accompaniment.

Choral music

Learners perform the gospel melody *Standing in the need of prayer* and add harmony parts that (a) move in parallel and (b) are modified to fit with conventional harmonies. They listen to gospel music from South Africa, London and the United States, focusing on ways in which changes of texture create variety and interest, and listen with a similar focus to traditional choral pieces from New Zealand, Bulgaria and Pakistan. Finally, they arrange a group performance of a gospel melody and compose their own a-cappela pieces incorporating idiomatic features of one of the styles which they have studied.

Story of an encounter or event

Learners tell a story in sound about an encounter between two or more cultures, or else in response to an event of local, national or international importance. They explain the original musical ideas, how they were developed and why some of the musical features were chosen. If songs are used, either familiar or specially composed, there is consideration, discussion and appraisal of pitch, duration, dynamics, diction and phrasing.

Personal, social and health education

Overview

It is in personal, social and health education (PSHE) and in citizenship education that the ideas and concepts discussed in chapter 2 are most likely to be taught directly. There can be recurring emphasis, in every aspect of PSHE, on shared humanity; difference, belonging and identity; achievements and excellence in many different settings and contexts; the local neighbourhood and its links with global systems; rights, conflict, justice and fairness; and race, racisms and racial justice.

PSHE qualities and skills are taught and learnt not only directly but also implicitly through the ways in which schools and classrooms are organised. Also, as discussed in other parts of this chapter, they can feature in all other curriculum subjects.

Commentary

Learners are expected by national requirements for PSHE to:

- recognise what they like and dislike, what is fair and unfair, and what is right and wrong

- share their opinions on things that matter to them and explain their views

- recognise, name and deal with their feelings in positive ways

- take part in discussions and debates

- agree and follow rules for the conduct of discussions

- appreciate that they belong to a range of groups and heritages

- understand what improves and what harms the natural and built environment

- recognise how their behaviour affects other people

- consider social and moral dilemmas in everyday life and in local, national and global politics.

The extract from a sermon to slaves in *Views and voices 51* is a poetic summary of the aims and concerns of PSHE. Similarly poetic, but in an entirely different kind of style, is the piece of writing in *Views and voices 52*.

Views and voices – 50

Open and free and curious

...If you help everyone else in your world to learn and understand about themselves and each other and the way everything works, and by showing them how to be kind instead of cruel, and patient instead of hasty, and cheerful instead of surly, and above all how to keep their minds open and free and curious...

The Amber Spyglass by Philip Pullman, 2000

Views and voices – 51

We here

Extracts from a sermon preached to slaves in nineteenth century America

Here, in this here place we flesh; flesh that weeps, laughs; flesh that dances on bare grass. Love it. Love it hard. Yonder they do not love your flesh. They despise it. They don't love your eyes; they'd just as soon pick em out. Nor do they love the skin on your back. Yonder they flay it. And O my people they do not love your hands. Those they only use, tie, bind, chop off and leave empty. Love your hands. Love them! Love them. Raise them up and kiss them. Raise them up and kiss them. Touch others with them, pat them together, stroke them on your face cos they don't love that either. You got to love it, *you!*

And no, they ain't in love with your mouth. Yonder, out there, they will see it broken and break it again. What you say out of it they will not heed. What you scream from it they do not hear. What you put into it to nourish your body they will snatch away and give you leavins instead. No, they don't love your mouth. *You* got to love it...

Beloved, by Toni Morrison, 1987

Schemes of work

In all programmes of PSHE there are ample opportunities to teach the key ideas outlined in chapter 2.

Views and voices – 52

All I really needed to know

All I really needed to know about how to live and what to do and how to be I learned in kindergarten. These are the things I learned:

- Share everything

- Play fair

- Don't hit people

- Put things back where you found them

- Clean up your own mess

- Don't take things that aren't yours

- Say you're sorry when you hurt somebody

- Wash your hands before you eat

- Flush

- Warm cookies and cold milk are good for you

- Live a balanced life – learn some and think some and draw and paint and sing and dance and play and work every day some

- Take a nap every afternoon.

- When you go out into the world, watch out for traffic, hold hands, and stick together

- Be aware of wonder

- Remember the little seed in the Styrofoam cup: The roots go down and the plant goes up and nobody really knows how or why, but we are all like that

- Goldfish and hamsters and white mice and even the little seed in the Styrofoam cup – they all die. So do we

- And then remember the Dick-and-Jane books and the first word you learned – the biggest word of all – LOOK.

Everything you need to know is in there somewhere. The Golden Rule and love and basic sanitation. Ecology and politics and equality and sound living.

All I Really Need To Know I Learned In Kindergarten, by Robert Fulghum, 1986

Classroom examples

Moral courage

Learners investigate the story of Rosa Parks and her role in the early days of the civil rights movement in the United States. (Useful books at key stages 1 and 2 include *The Bus Ride* by William Miller and *A Picture Book of Rosa Parks* by David Adler.) They discuss the concept of moral courage, using materials developed by the Anne Frank Trust UK and available at www.annefrank.org.uk, and make real or imagined entries for the Anne Frank Moral Courage Awards programme.

They sign up to the Anne Frank Declaration and create posters about this for the classroom and school corridors.

Identities

In groups learners research concepts of identity, belonging and community, using a range of sources of information, including the Britkids website. Each group feeds back to the rest of the class and discuss what they have found out and discuss diversity in Britain in the twenty-first century. Finally, each imagines identity as a mask that reflects aspects of heritage or community, and each learner designs and creates a mask to reflect their various loyalties and affiliations.

I too sing

Learners commit to memory the poem *I too sing America* by Langston Hughes, readily downloadable from the website of the Academy of American Poets at www.poets.org. They then write similar poems about themselves and their feelings about Britain and also write poems using other personas.

Sibel's story

Learners use a Persona doll to construct and tell the story of Sibel, a five year old child from Iran whose family is seeking asylum in the UK. Information is provided by the teacher about reasons for leaving Iran and the dangerous journey to the UK. Imaginary family photographs are found on the internet and culturally relevant artefacts such as clothing are obtained from friends. Commonalities between Sibel and the learners are established, for example with regard to the likes, dislikes and worries of any five year old girl in the world. As the story progresses there is consideration of cultural, linguistic and religious diversity.

(For further information and ideas, visit the website of Portsmouth Ethnic Minority Support Service at www.blss.portsmouth.sch.uk/default.htm.)

Physical education and dance

Overview

PE and dance are relevant to the themes discussed in chapter 2 when:

- skills in games, gymnastic and athletic activities and dance contribute to self esteem and a sure sense of personal identity and belonging

- there is increasing commitment to rules and fairness and to team spirit

- dance is used to explore and express aspects of personal and cultural identity, and justice, conflict and shared humanity

- examples of high achievement in gymnastics, athletics, sport and dance are taken from a wide range of countries and cultures.

Commentary

All learners should have opportunities to progress. At the same time there should be sensitivity to relevant differences amongst them. Progress is:

- from early explorations to acquiring and developing a range of skills that show improved control and coordination, and then to refining and extending these skills and being able to perform them with accuracy, consistency and fluency

- from the simple selection and application of skills, in a series or in combination, to the planning and use of more complex sequences, games, strategies and compositional principles

---

Views and voices – 53

The ethics of the game

... Rapidly we learnt to obey the umpire's decision without question, however irrational it was. We learned to play with the team, which meant subordinating your personal inclinations, and even interest, to the good of the whole. We kept a stiff upper lip in that we did not complain about ill-fortune. We did not denounce failures, but 'Well tried' or 'Hard luck' came easily to our lips. We were generous to opponents and congratulated them on victories, even when we knew they did not deserve it ... Two people lived in me: one, the rebel against all family and school discipline and order; the other, a Puritan, who would have cut off a finger sooner than do anything contrary to the ethics of the game.

C.L.R.James, 1963

Views and voices – 53

That noble game

It's the 1970s. Daud has recently arrived in England from East Africa. He goes into various pubs but is made unwelcome or is thrown out.

The most poignant exclusion was from The Cricketers, where he had gone two or three times and begun to feel safe. The photographs on the walls were a disappointment, honouring only English and Australian players. There were no Sir Garys and no Three Ws, but he found the cricket paraphernalia on the walls soothing. In the end the landlady had asked him to leave. She told him she could not be sure of restraining her husband from jumping over the bar and cracking him one. So he had gone, saddened and shaken that it was a lover of that noble game who had so misused him.

Abdulrazak Gurnah, *Pilgrim's Way*

- from being able to describe what learners see being performed to making simple evaluations of performance and being able to use this information to improve the quality of their work

- from knowing that exercise makes you hot or out of breath to developing an understanding of why an activity may be good for you and how important it is to your general health and wellbeing, and how different types of fitness affect your performance.

Activities and programmes should enable all learners to develop qualities and skills relating to cooperation and sensitivity, fair play and mutual respect, empathy, teamwork, attack and defence, acceptance of rules and rulings, management of conflict and confrontation, and handling success and failure with dignity. Cricket, referred to in *Views and voices 53* and *Views and voices 54*, is in certain respects representative of all games and sports.

It is through sport that many people develop a strong attachment to the town or city where they live and a sense of belonging and identity shared with people who in other respects are different from themselves. The point is well made in an autobiographical sketch by the Black British writer Caryl Philips, cited in *Views and voices 55*.

Review and development

On page 63, ten features of good practice in PE and dance are listed in order to guide reviews of current provision and to assist with planning further development.

Schemes of work

The national schemes of work for PE and dance are to do with activities (athletic, outdoor and adventurous, gymnastic, dance) and games (invasion, striking and fielding, net and wall), not content. They can therefore be used, if schools wish, with the themes outlined in chapter 2.

Classroom examples

Incident in the local press
In response to a range of stimuli (stories, music, newspapers, quotations, props and artefacts) learners use movement to express feelings, moods and ideas and then build up a narrative based on a news item in the local press about a racist incident.

'Football Unites Racism Divides'
Learners visit the anti-racism website of Sheffield United (www.furd.org.uk) and make a list of issues relating to the eradication of racism on football terraces and in football management. They draw up a code of conduct for themselves and choreograph a dance performance to illustrate and support it.

Fusion and belonging
Using skills and styles from classical and contemporary traditions, learners create a performance which explores issues of inclusion and ostracising in a friendship group, or in playground or street culture.

Skill and strategy
Learners play broadly similar games from two or more different cultures and note the similarities and variations in terms of skill, purpose and strategy.

Views and voices – 55

You will always be Leeds

Leeds United reminds me of my father. Leeds United reminds me of my best friend, John. Leeds United reminds me of the moment my mother caught me crying as a teenager because in 1972 Leeds had lost a game that would have given them the double. Leeds United reminds me of who I am. All together now, 'We are Leeds.' 'We are Leeds.' 'We are Leeds.' Somewhere, thirty-five years ago, a small black boy in the company of his white teenage babysitter stood on the terraces at Elland Road and muttered those words for the first time. And I say back to that child today, 'And you will always be Leeds, for they are a mirror in which you will see reflected the complexity that is your life.'

Caryl Phillips, 2001

Learners should appreciate that sport, games and movement are universal human activities, but also that there are many culturally specific ways of expressing the same values and aspirations. These points should be illustrated by posters and other visual resources that are drawn from a wide range of cultural and national settings.

Dance should be used as a medium through which learners explore and express aspects of their own identities, and feelings and views of current social issues.

Views and voices – 56

Quite slippery matter

When I first started working in Britain in the early 1980s, we were forced to be 'authentic Indians' ... This meant that you had to dance in a particular way ... To conform to the idea of being 'authentic', you had to fulfil certain very rigid ideas of what people expected of what was natural for an Indian to use. These notions were the product of a long history of preconceptions and dialogue between Britain and India ... The old colonial discourse is not dead, it is still very much alive and is very dangerous ... I think it is important that people see and listen to art that is dealing with quite slippery matter as well as the more reassuring classical forms. However, I am glad I was trained as classical dancer, it's a very useful resource.

Shobana Jeyasingh, British Council conference on Reinventing Britain, 1997

Religious education

Overview

Religious education is relevant to the principles and concepts discussed in chapter 2 when learners:

- interact with faith communities in their own local neighbourhood and see them within wider regional, national and international contexts

- are aware of substantial diversity and differences – theological, political, national, ethnic – within each world religion

- study the perspectives and ethical values of faith communities with regard to current political controversies

- give thought, in relation to issues of conflict and injustice, to whether religion is part of the problem or part of the solution.

Commentary

RE should enable learners to:

- acquire and develop knowledge and understanding of Christianity and the other principal religions represented in the UK

- develop understanding of the influence of beliefs, values and traditions on individuals, communities, societies and cultures

- make reasoned and informed judgements about religious and moral issues, with reference to the teachings of the principal religions represented in the UK

- enhance their spiritual, moral, social and cultural development by developing awareness of the fundamental questions of life raised by human experiences, and of how religious teachings can relate to them

---

Views and voices – 57

A kind of cleansing

We'd better acknowledge the sheer danger of religiousness. It can be a tool to reinforce diseased perceptions of reality, a way of teaching ourselves not to see the particular human agony in front of us; or worse, of teaching ourselves not to see ourselves, our violence, our actual guilt as opposed to our abstract 'religious' sinfulness. Our religious talking, seeing, knowing, needs a kind of cleansing.

Rowan Williams, 2002

Views and voices – 58

The little ones

God always sides with the little ones, children over adults, the sick over the healthy, the minorities over the powerful.

Sara Maitland, *Home Truths*

Views and voices – 59

This wretched word spiritual

She got hold of this wretched word 'spiritual'. It's one of those words I've never quite understood. I mean, I've always hated the way people use it. They use it to try to bump themselves up. 'Oh I've had a spiritual experience,' they say, as if that's the end of the argument. Spiritual, meaning: 'It's mine and shove off.' People use it to prove they're sensitive. They want to dignify quite ordinary things. Religion. Now that is something different. I like religion. Because religion has rules. It's based on something which actually occurred. There are things to believe in. And what's more, what makes it worth following – not that I do, mind you – there's some expectation of how you're meant to behave. But 'spiritual' ... well, it's all wishy-washy.

Skylight, by David Hare, 1997

- respond to such questions with reference to the teachings and practices of religions and other belief systems, relating them to their own understandings and experience

- reflect on their own beliefs, values and experiences in the light of their study

- develop positive attitudes towards people who hold views and beliefs different from their own, and towards living in a society of diverse religions.

At all key stages, learners:

- identify aspects of their own experience and feelings in religious material studied

- respond sensitively to the experiences and feelings of others, including those with a faith

- compare aspects of their own experiences and those of others, identifying what influences their lives

View and voices – 60

Let sleeping dogs lie?

To include issues of conflict and justice would not be difficult to arrange in an RE curriculum – for the religions of the world teem with issues of justice, equality and dignity. Less easy to provide is the willingness and the sensitivity and the courage required of teachers to handle such issues in an enlightening and creative way. The external constraints are many and the teacher will not embark on the venture in the face of negative answers to such questions as: Is it on the exam syllabus? Might the parents object? Can I open and close in a single period? Will it get them jobs? Will colleagues say (again) that RE is a waste of everyone's time? Am I sufficiently experienced to succeed in the venture? And these questions will come before the more searching ones such as: Where do I stand on colonialism and imperialism? What is its relationship with religion? Can I present religion as a force for peace in world affairs? Am I manipulating minds? Can I accept responsibility for the children's learning? Will they be creatively discontented or merely frustrated and bitter? Shall I let sleeping dogs die?

Angela Wood, 1984

- ask questions about the significant experiences of key figures from religions studied and suggest answers from their own and others' experiences, including believers

- make informed responses to questions of identity and experience in the light of their learning respond to the teachings and experience of inspirational people by relating these to their own and others' lives.

Religious education makes substantial demands on teachers, as recalled in *Views and voices 60*.

Schemes of work

QCA schemes of work relevant to the concepts and ideas discussed in chapter 2 include *What does it mean to belong?*, *Visiting a place of worship*, *What is faith and what difference does it make?*, *What religions are represented in our neighbourhood?*, *How do the beliefs of Christians influence their actions?*, *The role of the mosque*, *How do people express their faith through the arts?*, *What does justice mean for religious believers?*

Classroom examples

Problem or solution?
Learners debate three 'Big Myths' set out in *Connect: different faiths, shared values*, published by the Inter-Faith Network in association with TimeBank and the National Youth Agency in 2004. The myths are (1) 'Well, they may say they're religious but no-one believes any of that stuff' (2) 'Religious people are just a bunch of fanatics' and (3) 'Religion divides people – all the religions hate each other'. They then sort through some of the stories and case studies in the *Connect* booklet about practical inter-faith projects in various parts of Britain. For each project they ask and consider three questions: What do you see as the strengths of this project? What reservations or criticisms do you have? If you met someone from the project what would you ask them?

Reviewing a project
Learners research and study a project such as the Soul of Europe (www.soulofeurope.org), committed to rebuilding and repairing the Ferhadijah Mosque in Banja Luka, Bosnia. They list what they see as the strengths and advantages of the project; note any reservations or criticisms they may have; and list the questions they would like to ask if there were a chance of speaking and meeting with a representative of the project. Arising from such work, they draft guidelines on inter-faith dialogue and cooperation and then compare these with guidelines issued by the Inter-Faith Network (downloadable from www.interfaith.org.uk).

To be a British Muslim
Learners attend to the testimony and experience of young British Muslims, as outlined and discussed on the websites of *Muslim News, Q News* and the Muslim Council of Britain, and in the 2004 report of the Commission on British Muslims and Islamophobia. They identify commonalities, similarities and differences in the lives and identities of British Christians, British Jews, British Sikhs, and so on.

Christian action on racial justice
Learners obtain a copy of *Redeeming the Time: all God's people must challenge racism*, issued by the Churches Commission for Racial Justice (details in bibliography), and seek comment about it from local churches.

Jewish Perspectives
Learners study Jewish perspectives on racial justice, as presented in *Making a Difference* by Edie Friedman and *Let's Make a Difference: teaching antiracism in primary schools* by Edie Friedman, Hazel Woolfson, Sheila Freedman and Shirley Murgraff (details in bibliography) and interview members of the local Jewish community in order to obtain their views.

Science

Overview

Science is relevant to the big ideas and key concepts outlined in chapter 2 when:

- scientific skills and concepts are illustrated with regard to issues of global interdependence, shared humanity, difference, diversity, conflict and justice

- it is emphasised that science is a universal human achievement, not something which is distinctively western.

In addition, science involves skills of analysis, problem-solving and logical thought that are transferable to discussions of social, moral and political issues. The scientific concept of a fair test is applicable in a wide range of other fields besides science.

Commentary

A recurring key concept in all the sciences is interdependence. From KS1 onwards, for example, there is learning about ways in which animals and plants are suited to the environment in which they live; ways in which animals and plants depend on each other; and how relationships between living things affect populations of organisms. Such knowledge is the basis of ecology and a major component of sustainable development.

In every science topic there are opportunities to stress that science is a universal human activity and that there are example of high achievement in a wide range of countries and cultures.

In most science topics there are opportunities to consider the social, cultural and economic context in which scientific enquiry takes place and in which its discoveries are applied.

Views and voices – 61

A hundred centuries of trial and error

... We began studying physics together, and Sandro was surprised when I tried to explain to him some of the ideas that at the time I was confusedly cultivating. That the nobility of man, acquired in a hundred centuries of trial and error, lay in making himself the conqueror of matter, and that I had enrolled in chemistry because I wanted to remain faithful to this nobility. That conquering matter is to understand it, and understanding matter is necessary to understanding the universe and ourselves...

... Finally, and fundamentally, an honest and open boy, did he not smell the stench of Fascist truths which tainted the sky? Did he not perceive it as an ignominy that a thinking man should be asked to believe without thinking? Was he not filled with disgust at all the dogmas, all the unproved affirmations, all the imperatives?

He did feel it; so then, how could he not feel a new dignity and majesty in our study, how could he ignore the fact that the chemistry and physics on which we fed, besides nourishments vital in themselves, were the antidote to Fascism which he and I were seeking, because they were clear and distinct and verifiable at every step, and not a tissue of lies and emptiness, like the radio and newspapers?

Primo Levi, *The Periodic Table*, 1975. This part of the book is set in Italy in the 1930s.

Views and voices – 62

Use and conversion

People all over the world are involved in chemical processes, whether they be making soap and candles, purifying salt, brewing beer or wine, spreading fertilisers and weedkillers, washing clothes, bleaching hair, applying suntan lotion, developing films, glueing joints, patching an old car with fibreglass, or a host of other activities carried out for pleasure, profit or self-preservation. Valuing cultural diversity implies recognising the achievement of human beings in different cultural, historical and environmental settings, with particular reference to the use and conversion of raw materials by chemical means into usable products.

Iolo Wyn Evans, 1984

A final voice

The first of the *Views and voices* in this book ('Wild with the joy of it' on page 12) is about science and about humankind's shared environment. It is fitting that the final voice in the series should also be about science and similarly about the environment which all humans share.

Views and voices – 63

Eggshell delicacy

As scientists have pieced together the astonishing history of our cosmos – with the original explosion of hydrogen plasma accurately timed only in 1974 (some 10,000 million years after the event), what has emerged is the extraordinary delicacy and fragility of the systems through which organic life has been sustained on earth. Phytoplankton releasing oxygen, photosynthesis building up the planet's atmospheric shield, the billions of neurons in the human brain, the infinitely small structures of DNA, the double helix through which all the instructions are given to the cells of organic life – these mysteries of smallness are the gifts of science in the twentieth century. They emphasise not so much the vast and terrifying capacities of nature as the eggshell delicacy of the instruments which alone make the energies usable and safe.

Barbara Ward, 1976

Schemes of work

National schemes of work about shared humanity include *Ourselves* and *Health and growth at KS1*, *Keeping healthy* and *How we see things at KS2*, and *Food and digestion at KS3*. Principles of ecological interdependence are taught in *Ecological relationships, Habitats* and *Plants and synthesis at KS3*. Science as a universal human achievement is taught directly through *Investigating scientific questions* and indirectly, if teachers wish and intend this, in every scheme of work and module from KS1 onwards.

Classroom examples

Commonalities and differences

In a topic on *Ourselves*, learners make surveys of various physical characteristics, including skin colour, eye colour, gender and height, and of personal interests, for example favourite foods and pets, and draw Venn diagrams to show commonalities and differences.

The context of scientific invention

In a topic on *Electrical circuits* learners study the development of the electric lamp. They develop knowledge of the heating and lighting effect of a current; that resistance to a current depends on the type and thickness of the conducting material; that air is needed for things to burn (oxygen is the active ingredient); that the vacuum pump to remove air was invented; different materials were tested as filaments (eg metals, carbon); and that various techniques for holding the filaments were investigated.

Within this context learners study the contributions of the great African American inventor Lewis Latimer (1848-1928). Latimer devised a way of encasing the filament within a cardboard envelope which prevented the carbon from breaking and thereby provided a much longer life to the bulb and hence made the bulbs less expensive and more efficient. This enabled electric lighting to be installed in homes and throughout streets. Learners become aware of the nature of scientific enquiry; the creativity, rivalries and competition involved in scientific invention and discovery; the cultural, social, economic and industrial circumstances in which scientific progress takes place and by which it is influenced; the struggle for due recognition of black inventors; and the nature and effects of institutional racism.

The spread of knowledge

Learners play a version of the game *Woolly Thinking* in order to study the spread of knowledge in the year 1000. The game vividly illustrates and dramatises interactions between China, India, the Middle East and Europe and portrays science as a universal human activity. Full details and instructions can be found on the website of the Muslim Home School Network, based in the United States, at http://www.muslimhomeschool.com – click on Pride and then on educational material. Learners then explore the wealth of material about Muslim science at www.muslimheritage.com and the implications of such material for any British classroom in the 21st century at the website of the Islamic Society of Britain (www.isb.org.uk and follow the links to the Virtual Classroom.)

4 HOW ARE WE DOING?
Questions for review and development

This chapter, like the previous chapter, considers each curriculum subject or area in turn. The emphasis here, however, is on reviewing and assessing current practice in a school and on identifying (a) strengths in current provision and (b) gaps and omissions. For each subject a questionnaire is provided for staff to fill in and – more especially and more valuably – to discuss. Many of the items in the questionnaires are identical or almost identical across several different subjects.

Each proforma on the following pages has the same format. There is a list of features of good practice, and staff are invited to consider how they would rate their school's stage of development along a five-point scale, using a simple code as follows:

0 – the feature is not present
1 – we are beginning to focus
2 – making satisfactory progress
3 – good
4 – excellent

In the right hand column of each proforma staff are invited to indicate evidence for their self-assessment and to write notes on next steps.

Art and design
Review and development

Features of good practice	Stage of development	Evidence and suggestions for development
1. Achievement everywhere Examples of artistic excellence are taken from a range of cultural traditions over the centuries and not only from European traditions.		
2. Interactions and influences There is stress on ways in which artists from different cultures and traditions have borrowed from each other and influenced each other.		
3. Shared humanity There is stress on common elements, concerns and strivings in different cultures, reflecting universal human values, questions and concerns.		
4. Visitors Visiting artists who come to the school – painters, potters, printmakers – are from a range of cultures and traditions.		
5. Social issues There is reference to the ways in which artists explore current social issues through their work.		
6. Personal identity Through a variety of art forms learners explore and express aspects of their own personal and cultural identity.		
7. Display Art on display in corridors and other public areas reflects the features of good practice listed above.		
8. Lesson planning Lesson planning proformas contain prompts for considering how issues such as those listed above will be included.		
9. Training Continuing professional development of staff includes consideration of the features of good practice listed above.		
10. Responsibility A member of staff has responsibility for keeping the art and design curriculum under review with regard to the features of good practice listed above.		

In the column headed Stage of development please use the following code:
0 – the feature is not present; 1 – beginning to focus; 2 – making satisfactory progress; 3 – good; 4 – excellent.

In the right hand column, write notes on (a) evidence for the grade that is proposed and (b) ideas and suggestions for further development and action.

Citizenship
Review and development

Features of good practice	Stage of development	Evidence and suggestions for development
1. Achievement everywhere Examples of successful change and social organisation are taken from a range of societies and not only from Britain.		
2. Influences and interaction There is stress on ways in which different societies and communities borrow from each other and influence each other.		
3. Shared humanity There is stress on common elements, concerns and strivings in different cultures, reflecting universal human values, questions and concerns.		
4. Race and racisms Learners become acquainted with concepts of racism and race equality, multiculturalism, justice and fairness, and social inclusion.		
5. Personal identity Both orally and in writing learners explore and express aspects of their own personal, cultural and national identity.		
6. Strategies of change Learners study campaigns and movements for greater justice and appreciate the advantages and disadvantages of different kinds of strategy and method.		
7. Collective decisions Learners acquire and practise skills of collective decision-making both in the classroom and the school community.		
8. Lesson planning Lesson planning proformas contain prompts for considering how issues such as those listed above will be included.		
9. Training Continuing professional development of staff includes consideration of the features of good practice listed above.		
10. Responsibility A member of staff has responsibility for keeping the citizenship curriculum under review with regard to the features of good practice listed above.		

In the column headed Stage of development please use the following code:
0 – the feature is not present; 1 – beginning to focus; 2 – making satisfactory progress; 3 – good; 4 – excellent.

In the right hand column, write notes on (a) evidence for the grade that is proposed and (b) ideas and suggestions for further development and action.

Design and technology
Review and development

Features of good practice	Stage of development	Evidence and suggestions for development
1. Achievement everywhere Examples of technological achievement are taken from a range of cultural traditions over the centuries and not only from European societies.		
2. Influences and interaction There is stress on ways in which different cultures, countries and traditions have borrowed from each other's technology and have influenced each other.		
3. Shared humanity There is stress on common elements, concerns and strivings in different cultures, reflecting universal human values, questions and concerns.		
4. Universality Principles of design are seen as universal, used in all cultures and traditions.		
5. Social issues There is reference to the ways in which technology is bound up with issues of power, conflict and fairness within and between societies		
6. Materials and resources Software, assignments and resources reflect aspects of multi-ethnic Britain and global society.		
7. Visits Visits to or from the school relating to D & T involve meetings and encounters with people from a range of different ethnic and cultural backgrounds.		
8. Lesson planning Lesson planning proformas contain prompts for considering how issues such as those listed above will be included.		
9. Training Continuing professional development of staff includes consideration of the features of good practice listed above.		
10. Responsibility A member of staff has responsibility for keeping the design and technology curriculum under review with regard to the features of good practice listed above.		

In the column headed Stage of development please use the following code:
0 – the feature is not present; 1 – beginning to focus; 2 – making satisfactory progress; 3 – good; 4 – excellent.

In the right hand column, write notes on (a) evidence for the grade that is proposed and (b) ideas and suggestions for further development and action.

English
Review and development

Features of good practice	Stage of development	Evidence and suggestions for development
1. Achievement everywhere Texts and theatrical forms are taken from a range of cultural traditions over the centuries, not from Europe only.		
2. Influences and interaction There is stress on ways in which writers from different cultures, countries and traditions have borrowed from each other and influenced each other.		
3. Shared humanity There is stress on common elements, concerns and strivings in different cultures, reflecting universal human values, questions and concerns.		
4. Bias and stereotyping Learners study aspects of bias in literature, drama and the media and learn to recognise stereotypes.		
5. Social issues There is reference to the ways in which fiction, poetry and drama explore current social issues through their work.		
6. Varieties of language Learners study differences between formal and informal language, and nuances of meaning between different words.		
7. Personal identity In writing, orally and through drama, learners explore and express aspects of their own personal and cultural identity.		
8. Lesson planning Lesson planning proformas contain prompts for considering how issues such as those listed above will be included.		
9. Training Continuing professional development of staff includes consideration of the features of good practice listed above.		
10. Responsibility A member of staff has responsibility for keeping the English curriculum under review with regard to the features of good practice listed above.		

In the column headed Stage of development please use the following code:
0 – the feature is not present; 1 – beginning to focus; 2 – making satisfactory progress; 3 – good; 4 – excellent.

In the right hand column, write notes on (a) evidence for the grade that is proposed and (b) ideas and suggestions for further development and action.

Geography
Review and development

Features of good practice	Stage of development	Evidence and suggestions for development
1. Achievement everywhere Examples of successful relationships with the physical environment are taken from all parts of the world.		
2. Influences and interaction There is stress on ways in which people from different cultures, countries and habitats have borrowed from each other and influenced each other.		
3. Shared humanity There is stress on common elements, concerns and strivings in different cultures, reflecting universal human values, questions and concerns.		
4. Bias and stereotyping Negative images of other countries and cultures are avoided or criticised.		
5. Materials and resources Tasks, assignments and resources reflect aspects of multi-ethnic Britain and global society.		
6. Social issues The relevance of geographical concepts to current social issues and controversies is clearly seen.		
7. School linking Work in geography features in school-linking schemes with schools in other countries.		
8. Lesson planning Lesson planning proformas contain prompts for considering how issues such as those listed above will be included.		
9. Training Continuing professional development of staff includes consideration of the features of good practice listed above.		
10. Responsibility A member of staff has responsibility for keeping the geography curriculum under review with regard to the features of good practice listed above.		

In the column headed Stage of development please use the following code:
0 – the feature is not present; 1 – beginning to focus; 2 – making satisfactory progress; 3 – good; 4 – excellent.

In the right hand column, write notes on (a) evidence for the grade that is proposed and (b) ideas and suggestions for further development and action.

History
Review and development

Features of good practice	Stage of development	Evidence and suggestions for development
1. Achievement everywhere Examples of successful social organisation and change are taken from a range of societies and not only from Britain.		
2. Influences and interaction There is stress on ways in which different cultures, countries and societies have borrowed from each other and influenced each other.		
3. Interdependence There is stress on the relationship between British history and the history of other countries and societies.		
4. Shared humanity There is stress on common elements, concerns and strivings in different societies, reflecting universal human values, questions and concerns.		
5. Bias and stereotyping Learners study bias in accounts and narratives about the past and recognise stereotypes.		
6. Impact of the past There is reference to the ways in which events in the past have affected current issues and controversies.		
7. Varieties of Britishness Learners study concepts and aspects of British identity over the centuries, and differences of region, nation, gender, class, religion and ethnicity.		
8. Lesson planning Lesson planning proformas contain prompts for considering how issues such as those listed above will be included.		
9. Training Continuing professional development of staff includes consideration of the features of good practice listed above.		
10. Responsibility A member of staff has responsibility for keeping the history curriculum under review with regard to the features of good practice listed above.		

In the column headed Stage of development please use the following code:
0 – the feature is not present; 1 – beginning to focus; 2 – making satisfactory progress; 3 – good; 4 – excellent.

In the right hand column, write notes on (a) evidence for the grade that is proposed and (b) ideas and suggestions for further development and action.

Information and Communication Technology
Review and development

Features of good practice	Stage of development	Evidence and suggestions for development
1. Personal identity and views Learners frequently present and share personal opinions, viewpoints and ideas using text, images and sounds.		
2. Social, political and environmental issues Learners frequently use ICT in order to research and evaluate current social, political and environmental issues.		
3. Cultural diversity Learners frequently use ICT in order to research and evaluate a range of viewpoints, perspectives and points of view.		
4. Range of views Through email and on-line forums learners contact people throughout the world and encounter a range of views and perspectives on every subject.		
5. School-linking ICT is used in school-linking schemes.		
6. Critical evaluation There is critical evaluation of websites specialising in social and racial justice issues.		
7. Curriculum support ICT is used to support citizenship education and PSHE, particularly with regard to issues of race, racisms and racial justice		
8. Lesson planning Lesson planning proformas contain prompts for considering how issues such as those listed above will be included.		
9. Training Continuing professional development of staff includes consideration of the features of good practice listed above.		
10. Responsibility A member of staff has responsibility for keeping the ICT curriculum under review with regard to the features of good practice listed above.		

In the column headed Stage of development please use the following code:
0 – the feature is not present; 1 – beginning to focus; 2 – making satisfactory progress; 3 – good; 4 – excellent.

In the right hand column, write notes on (a) evidence for the grade that is proposed and (b) ideas and suggestions for further development and action.

Mathematics
Review and development

Features of good practice	Stage of development	Evidence and suggestions for development
1. Achievement everywhere Examples of mathematical achievement are taken from a range of cultural traditions over the centuries and not only from European culture.		
2. Influences and interaction There is stress on ways in which mathematicians from different cultures, countries and traditions have borrowed from each other and influenced each other.		
3. Shared humanity There is stress on common elements, concerns and strivings in different cultures, reflecting universal human values, questions and concerns.		
4. Universal language Mathematics is seen as a universal language, used in all cultures and traditions		
5. Social issues There is reference to the ways in which mathematics is required to explore and analyse current social issues.		
6. Materials, tasks and resources Tasks, assignments and resources reflect aspects of multi-ethnic Britain and global society.		
7. School linking Work in mathematics features in school-linking schemes with schools in other countries		
8. Lesson planning Lesson planning proformas contain prompts for considering how issues such as those listed above will be included.		
9. Training Continuing professional development of staff includes consideration of the features of good practice listed above.		
10. Responsibility A member of staff has responsibility for keeping the mathematics curriculum under review with regard to the features of good practice listed above.		

In the column headed Stage of development please use the following code:
0 – the feature is not present; 1 – beginning to focus; 2 – making satisfactory progress; 3 – good; 4 – excellent.

In the right hand column, write notes on (a) evidence for the grade that is proposed and (b) ideas and suggestions for further development and action.

Modern foreign languages
Review and development

Features of good practice	Stage of development	Evidence and suggestions for development
1. Diversity within diversity Examples of the target language are taken from a wide spectrum, not only from Europe.		
2. Influences and interaction There is stress on ways in which languages have borrowed from each other and influenced each other.		
3. Shared humanity There is stress on common elements, concerns and strivings in different cultures, reflecting universal human values, questions and concerns.		
4. Positive attitudes Learners develop positive attitudes towards the cultures and societies in which the target language is spoken.		
5. Materials and resources Tasks, assignments and resources reflect aspects of multi-ethnic societies throughout the world.		
6. Varieties of language Learners study differences between formal and informal language, and nuances of meaning between different words.		
7. Personal identity Both in writing and orally learners explore and express aspects of their own personal and cultural identity.		
8. Lesson planning Lesson planning proformas contain prompts for considering how issues such as those listed above will be included.		
9. Training Continuing professional development of staff includes consideration of the features of good practice listed above.		
10. Responsibility A member of staff has responsibility for keeping the MFL curriculum under review with regard to the features of good practice listed above.		

In the column headed Stage of development please use the following code:
0 – the feature is not present; 1 – beginning to focus; 2 – making satisfactory progress; 3 – good; 4 – excellent.

In the right hand column, write notes on (a) evidence for the grade that is proposed and (b) ideas and suggestions for further development and action.

Music
Review and development

Features of good practice	Stage of development	Evidence and suggestions for development
1. Achievement everywhere Examples of musical excellence are taken from a range of cultural traditions over the centuries, not only from European music.		
2. Influences and interaction There is stress on ways in which composers from different cultures and traditions have borrowed from each other and influenced each other.		
3. Shared humanity There is stress on common elements, concerns and strivings in different cultures, reflecting universal human values, questions and concerns.		
4. Visitors Visiting musicians who come to the school are from a range of cultures and traditions.		
5. Social issues There is reference to the ways in which composers and performers explore current social issues through their work.		
6. Personal identity Through a variety of musical forms learners explore and express aspects of their own personal and cultural identity.		
7. Cultural identity There is reference to the role of music in expressing, constructing and strengthening cultural and national identity.		
8. Lesson planning Lesson planning proformas contain prompts for considering how issues such as those listed above will be included.		
9. Training Continuing professional development of staff includes consideration of the features of good practice listed above.		
10. Responsibility A member of staff has responsibility for keeping the music curriculum under review with regard to the features of good practice listed above.		

In the column headed Stage of development please use the following code:
0 – the feature is not present; 1 – beginning to focus; 2 – making satisfactory progress; 3 – good; 4 – excellent.

In the right hand column, write notes on (a) evidence for the grade that is proposed and (b) ideas and suggestions for further development and action.

Personal, social and health education
Review and development

Features of good practice	Stage of development	Evidence and suggestions for development
1. Personal identity Both orally and in writing learners explore and express aspects of their own personal, cultural and national identity.		
2. Influences and interaction There is stress on ways in which different societies and communities borrow from each other and influence each other.		
3. Shared humanity There is stress on common elements, concerns and strivings in different cultures, reflecting universal human values, questions and concerns.		
4. Race and racisms Learners become acquainted with concepts of racism and race equality, multiculturalism, justice and fairness, and social inclusion.		
5. Local and global Learners see their locality and neighbourhood within the wider international context.		
6. Bullying Learners draw up rules and procedures for dealing with bullying and racist remarks and behaviour.		
7. Prejudice and bias There is study of how prejudices arise and their consequences and of ways of preventing and addressing them.		
8. Lesson planning Lesson planning proformas contain prompts for considering how issues such as those listed above will be included.		
9. Training Continuing professional development of staff includes consideration of the features of good practice listed above.		
10. Responsibility A member of staff has responsibility for keeping the PSHE curriculum under review with regard to the features of good practice listed above.		

In the column headed Stage of development please use the following code:
0 – the feature is not present; 1 – beginning to focus; 2 – making satisfactory progress; 3 – good; 4 – excellent.

In the right hand column, write notes on (a) evidence for the grade that is proposed and (b) ideas and suggestions for further development and action.

Physical education and dance
Review and development

Features of good practice	Stage of development	Evidence and suggestions for development
1. Sensitivity Account is taken of cultural preferences and requirements, for example to do with single sex provision, public performance, clothing, modesty, dancing, diet and fasting.		
2. Universals and differences Learners appreciate that sport, games and movement are universal human activities, but also that there are many culturally specific ways of expressing the same values and aspirations.		
3. Diversity Posters and other visual resources are drawn from a wide range of cultural and national settings.		
4. Fairness and rules Parallels are drawn between fairness and rules in games and fairness and games in society.		
5. Identity Dance is used to explore aspects of personal and cultural identity.		
6. Social issues Dance is used to express and explore views, feelings and stories to do with conflict and justice.		
7. Influence and interaction There is stress on ways different dance forms and traditions have influenced each other.		
8. Lesson planning Lesson planning proformas contain prompts for considering how issues such as those listed above will be included.		
9. Training Continuing professional development of staff includes consideration of the features of good practice listed above.		
10. Responsibility A member of staff has responsibility for keeping the PE curriculum under review with regard to the features of good practice listed above.		

In the column headed Stage of development please use the following code:
0 – the feature is not present; 1 – beginning to focus; 2 – making satisfactory progress; 3 – good; 4 – excellent.

In the right hand column, write notes on (a) evidence for the grade that is proposed and (b) ideas and suuggestions for further development and action.

Religious education
Review and development

Features of good practice	Stage of development	Evidence and suggestions for development
1. Achievement everywhere Examples of insights in Christianity and other religions are taken from a range of societies and cultures.		
2. Influences and interaction There is stress on ways in which different faiths, denominations and traditions have borrowed from each other and influenced each other.		
3. Shared humanity There is stress on common elements, concerns and strivings in different faiths, reflecting universal human values, questions and concerns.		
4. Visitors Visitors who come to the school to speak about their faith are from a range of cultures and traditions.		
5. Social issues There is reference to the ways in which religions address current social and moral issues.		
6. Personal identity In their encounter with religious traditions learners explore and express aspects of their own personal, religious and cultural identity.		
7. Problem and solution Learners study ways and situations in which religion can be part of the problem as well as of the solution.		
8. Lesson planning Lesson planning proformas contain prompts for considering how issues such as those listed above will be included.		
9. Training Continuing professional development of staff includes consideration of the features of good practice listed above.		
10. Responsibility A member of staff has responsibility for keeping the RE curriculum under review with regard to the features of good practice listed above.		

In the column headed Stage of development please use the following code:
0 – the feature is not present; 1 – beginning to focus; 2 – making satisfactory progress; 3 – good; 4 – excellent.

In the right hand column, write notes on (a) evidence for the grade that is proposed and (b) ideas and suggestions for further development and action.

Science
Review and development

Features of good practice	Stage of development	Evidence and suggestions for development
1. Achievement everywhere Examples of scientific achievement are taken from a range of cultural traditions over the centuries and not only from European culture.		
2. Influences and interaction There is stress on ways in which scientists from different cultures, countries and traditions have borrowed from each other and influenced each other.		
3. Shared humanity There is stress on common elements, concerns and strivings in different cultures, reflecting universal human values, questions and concerns.		
4. Universality Scientific methods and outlooks are seen as universal, used in all cultures and traditions.		
5. Social issues There is reference to the ways in which science is required to explore and analyse current social issues.		
6. Materials and resources Tasks, assignments and resources reflect aspects of multi-ethnic Britain and global society.		
7. School linking Work in science features in school-linking schemes with schools in other countries.		
8. Lesson planning Lesson planning proformas contain prompts for considering how issues such as those listed above will be included.		
9. Training Continuing professional development of staff includes consideration of the features of good practice listed above.		
10. Responsibility A member of staff has responsibility for keeping the science curriculum under review with regard to the features of good practice listed above.		

In the column headed Stage of development please use the following code:
0 – the feature is not present; 1 – beginning to focus; 2 – making satisfactory progress; 3 – good; 4 – excellent.

In the right hand column, write notes on (a) evidence for the grade that is proposed and (b) ideas and suggestions for further development and action.

5 PLAYGROUND AND STAFFROOM
ethos and relationships

The previous three chapters are about the content of the curriculum. Here, the concern is with the behaviour of learners in the playground and on journeys to and from school, and with whole-school policies and procedures.

Racism and bullying

Things people say

'Children and teenagers are forever trading insults with each other, it's part of everyday banter and good humour. It doesn't do lasting harm and in any case they grow out of it.'

'It's political correctness gone mad to claim a term such as Paki or Gyppo is worse than fatty or four eyes.'

'The man who runs my local corner shop is Asian and he calls it a Paki shop. So if he doesn't mind the word, why should I?'

'Children don't understand what they're saying when they use racist name-calling. It's totally unfair to punish them.'

'It's the parents we should challenge, not the children. But that's easier said than done. And anyway, do we have the right to challenge parents? The BNP is a legitimate political party, after all.'

'Well, I suppose we have to record racist incidents, since the government requires it. But it's not fair – there are lots of other bad things children do and say, some of them worse than racism, yet we don't have to record and report them.'

'Talking about racism makes minority children feel even more vulnerable and insecure and makes white children feel guilty and resentful. It causes more problems than it solves.'

Remarks such as these are sometimes made by teachers, parents and governors. Such attitudes and views often receive tacit or explicit support in the media. It is important that all staff – including lunch-time supervisors and other administrative staff – should feel that they can respond confidently and sensitively and, if necessary, robustly.

One place to start one's thinking is to identify (a) the similarities and (b) the differences between racist incidents and other kinds of bullying. This can be done as a group discussion exercise at a staff training session. Staff brainstorm two lists and then compare and contrast their own views with the points set out opposite.

Similarities

Ways in which racist behaviour and bullying are similar to each other

☐ Pupils who are targeted experience great distress. They may become miserable, fearful and depressed and their progress at school may be severely hampered.

☐ The distress is connected with feelings of being excluded and rejected.

☐ Also, the distress is because a characteristic is picked out which the person attacked can do nothing about – their size, whether they wear glasses, the colour of their hair, the colour of their skin, their religious or cultural background, and so on.

☐ Offenders may develop a false pride in their own strength and superiority.

☐ Teachers and even parents are sometimes not aware of the miseries that are being inflicted, or of the cruelty that is being perpetrated.

☐ When dealing with incidents, staff must attend to (a) the needs, feelings and wishes of pupils who are attacked (b) the needs, feelings and wishes of their parents and carers (c) the offenders or ringleaders responsible for the offending behaviour and (c) any bystanders and witnesses.

Differences

Ways in which racist behaviour and bullying are different from each other

☐ Racism has a long history affecting millions of people and is a common feature in wider society. People are seriously harmed and injured on account of it, and sometimes even viciously attacked and murdered. It is erroneous to think that children grow out of it – they do not!

☐ The law of the land recognises the seriousness of racism by requiring that courts impose higher sentences when an offence is aggravated by racist or religious hostility.

☐ The distinctive feature of a racist attack or insult is that a person is attacked not as an individual, as in most other offences, but as the representative of a family, community or group. This has three particularly harmful consequences:

• Other members of the same group, family or community are made to feel threatened and intimidated as well. So it is not just the pupil who is attacked who feels unwelcome or marginalised. 'When they call me a Paki,' explains nine-year-old Sereena, 'it's not just me they're hurting. It's all my family and all other black people too.'

• Racist words and behaviour are experienced as attacks on the values, loyalties and commitments central to a person's sense of identity and self-worth.

• Racist attacks are committed not only against a community but also, in the eyes of offenders themselves, on behalf of a community – offenders see themselves as representative of, and supported in their racism by, their friends, family and peer group.

Critical incidents

Stories such as those shown on the opposite page have the following uses:

■ If used near the start of a course or meeting, they give participants reassurance that the programme ahead is going to be down-to-earth, and that it is likely to help them solve or manage the practical problems of their everyday work.

■ They encode challenging ideas and arguments, and therefore encourage debate and disagreement.

■ They provide a useful reminder that even the best prepared plans can go wrong, and that unforeseen problems often arise. Successful change in education, as in other areas of work, requires amongst other things that there should be frank acknowledgement of uncertainties and failures, and realistic anticipation of resistance and difficulty.

■ They provide pegs on which to hang theoretical discussion, and therefore they make communication easier. They can be referred to directly during a course, for example in talks and lectures, and also in conversation.

■ By omitting much basic detail, they invite discussion of underlying issues and causes, and of long-term plans for whole-school change or development.

■ They invite attention to the ways in which they themselves are constructed and narrated. Has the person telling the story misunderstood his or her situation? How might a different person narrate the same episode?

■ They encourage a spirit of collaborative enquiry, such that participants feel keen to find out more, and to think more deeply, about underlying issues. They therefore provide a useful introduction to study of other kinds of material, for example the material later in this chapter headed *Defining and recording* and *Dealing with offenders*.

For each story the basic structure for discussion should be as follows:

❒ What might happen next, and what could be the consequences?

❒ What might or should happen in the medium term and the long term?

❒ What may have happened in the last few minutes?

❒ What factors are in the background and context, both in place and time?

❒ What principles can be derived from our discussion for dealing with incidents such as this?

On page 80 there are notes on the stories opposite, showing the main points that are likely to come out in discussion. It is often useful, when a small group discusses such stories, if one member of the group has responsibility for facilitating the discussion and if he or she consults, before and during the discussion, a brief commentary of the kind shown on page 80.

WHAT HAPPENS NEXT?

A bit of teasing

I'm the only Asian teacher at my school. During the war in Iraq a pupil who's also Asian told me that she was being teased by other pupils. 'We killed hundreds of your lot yesterday ... Saddam's your dad, innit ... we're getting our revenge for what you Pakis did to us on 11 September...' I asked her if she had told her class teacher. Yes, she had told her teacher, and her teacher had said: 'Never mind, it's not serious. They'll soon get over it. You'll have to expect a bit of teasing at a time like this.'

Not fair

A pupil was complaining to me bitterly earlier today. 'All right, I'm overweight and I'm not proud of it. But it really gets to me when other kids go on about it. Last week I lost it. I was out of order, right, but when these two kids said I was fatter than a Teletubby and twice as stupid I swore at them and used the word Paki. I got done for racism and was excluded for a day and my parents were informed and all, and I'm really pissed off, and nothing at all has happened to the kids who wound me up. It's not fair.'

Not surprising

I mentioned to a pupil's mother that in a PSHE lesson her son had made some unacceptably negative and extreme remarks about people seeking asylum. 'Well unfortunately it's not at all surprising,' she said. 'The fact is, my husband is an active member of the BNP.'

Hasn't come to school

I'm in Year 6. Yesterday there was a netball match against another school. I was in our team, so was Sue, my best friend. She's the only black pupil at our school. In the changing room before the match a girl in the other team said when she saw Sue, 'Oh, I thought we'd come to play netball, not to watch Planet of the Apes.' Sue was upset, particularly since there were some sniggers from other members of our own team. The insult was repeated and before I could do or say anything Sue threw a ball hard into the girl's face and caused a really spectacular nose bleed. The teacher from our school who was with us was furious, wouldn't listen to a word from Sue and sent her home. Today, Sue hasn't come to school.

Get on with your work

In October 2001 I had occasion to observe a colleague's Year 8 RE lesson. The students were copying pictures of Hindu deities into their books. 'These are the people who crashed the planes into the twin towers, aren't they, miss' said a boy. 'No,' she replied. 'That was Muslims, we're doing Hindus. Just get on with your work.'

Doesn't seem fair

At a governors' meeting the other day we received a report about religious education. 'What I object to,' said someone, 'is that these people who belong to other religions don't teach about Christianity in their own countries. So why should we teach about their religions in England? I know it's the law, but it doesn't seem fair, does it.' Some one else said, 'hear, hear'.

There are notes on these stories on page 80.

Defining and recording

Ofsted is required to inspect and comment on the measures which schools adopt to prevent incidents of racism occurring, and the measures they take when, despite their best efforts, incidents do occur. When carrying out this duty, Ofsted inspectors have to use the strict definition of a racist incident that was proposed by the Stephen Lawrence Inquiry report in 1999. Similarly schools are expected to use this definition.

It is important that all teachers, and also all support and administrative staff, should know what the official definition of a racist incident is, and why it has to be used. The official definition is this: *'any incident which is perceived to be racist by the victim or any other person'*. The term 'racism' refers to: *'conduct or words or practices which disadvantage or advantage people because of their colour, culture or ethnic origin'*.

A useful working definition in schools is:

> *Behaviour or language that makes a pupil feel unwelcome or marginalised because of their colour, ethnicity, culture, religion or national origin.*

There are four important points to stress about this definition:

- It is for the purposes of initial recording. Just because an incident is alleged or perceived to be racist does not mean that it necessarily is racist. But it does mean that it must be recorded and that an investigation must be carried out.

- Whether or not the offender intended their behaviour to be racist is irrelevant. Of course, when it comes to dealing with an incident the offender's intentions are an important consideration. But at the stage of initial recording and investigating, the offender's attitudes, motivation and awareness are not the main issue.

- A racist insult may refer to issues of culture or religion as well as to colour and appearance. Anti-Muslim insults and name-calling, for example, should be seen as racist. So should name-calling which targets the Gypsy Traveller community.

- A key concept is marginalising and excluding: a racist comment or act has the effect of making someone feel, or is intended to make someone feel, marginalised, excluded or unwelcome

In schools, incidents which may be perceived to be racist are mostly to do with verbal abuse, name-calling and insults. There may also be physical attacks and bullying; ostracising, freezing out and excluding from friendship groups; refusing to work with another pupil or to sit next to them; graffiti; damage to personal property; ridicule or exaggerated criticism of someone's cultural or religious background and traditions; and the distribution or display of offensive publications and symbols.

Of these, exclusion from a friendship group is common and yet is difficult to prove, since it does not necessarily involve the use of abusive language or of physical aggression.

Schools should keep records of racist incidents, and have to make an annual or termly report to their local authority. Even apparently trivial and low-level incidents should be recorded, for they may be part of a pattern or trend and may in any case have caused severe distress. Records should indicate the kind of investigation that was made following an allegation or perception of a racist incident, and whether the investigation found that the incident was indeed racist in its intentions and/or its effects.

On the opposite page there is a list of statements that could appear in Ofsted reports about good practice in individual schools. The list can be used to review current practice and is similar in this respect to the lists that appear in chapter 4 ('How are we doing?').

A note on semantics

Many documents and discussions about bullying and racist incidents in schools refer to 'perpetrators' and 'victims'. Both terms are unsatisfactory. The word victim is best avoided since it implies passivity, and ignores the feelings, wishes and emotional hurt of the person concerned. A further problem is that schools may think that they only need to record and report incidents when there is an identifiable person who has been attacked or hurt. The word perpetrator came into use at a time when the criminal justice system did not explicitly recognise racism as an aggravating factor, and for this reason the more obvious term offender was not available. Nowadays, however, it is widely recognised by the law of the land that racist behaviour is an offence. The more familiar and precise term offender is therefore preferable.

WHOLE-SCHOOL POLICY AND APPROACHES
A checklist of good practice on dealing with racist incidents

1. There is shared understanding amongst staff – including support and administrative staff as well as teachers – of ways in which bullying based on background, colour, religion or heritage is both similar to and different from other kinds of bullying.

2. There is the same shared understanding amongst pupils, parents and governors.

3. There is a code of practice which clearly outlines specific procedures to be followed for recording and dealing with racist incidents, as also with other kinds of abuse and bullying, on the school premises, and on journeys to and from school.

4. The governors take seriously their responsibility to report regularly to the LEA the number and nature of racist incidents at their school, and they indicate in their reports how the incidents were dealt with.

5. There is a history of taking reports seriously and following them up.

6. A user-friendly leaflet has been provided for pupils and their parents on what to do if they experience racism against them.

7. Pupils are involved in mediating in disputes, and in making clear that racist remarks and behaviour are unacceptable. They support each other in being assertive, as distinct from aggressive or submissive, when incidents occur.

8. All staff are vigilant with regard to behaviour amongst pupils, and ensure that they are as familiar as possible with pupils' experiences of bullying and racist incidents. For example, pupils have opportunities to report racist incidents anonymously, if they wish.

9. There are periodic surveys of pupils' experiences and perceptions of racism, using questionnaires and discussion groups, and involving people from outside the school if appropriate.

10. Staff accept that they have a responsibility to help ensure that play and leisure areas encourage and promote positive and co-operative behaviour amongst pupils.

11. The general ethos of the school (displays, assemblies, some of the examples across the curriculum) reflects and affirms diversity of language, culture, religion and appearance.

12. The school is involved from time to time in national projects such as Kick Racism Out Of Football, One World Week, Black History Month and Refugee Week.

13. There is coverage within the curriculum of interpersonal behaviour amongst pupils, including racist name-calling and bullying, and this is linked with wider issues of citizenship and participation in society.

14. There is coverage within the curriculum of key concepts such as colour racism and cultural racism, and institutional and individual racism, and of measures and campaigns to build racial justice.

Dealing with offenders

In the mid 1990s the Home Office funded research into the nature and extent of racist harassment. The researchers found that offenders are frequently children and young people of school age, and in this connection they provided 'offender profiles' for primary and secondary pupils respectively. Extracts from the profiles are shown below.

Primary school age

Racism is part of the language with which offenders have grown up – grandparents, parents, relatives, elder siblings hold, and regularly express, racist views. The recurring notion is that people who are not white 'do not belong here' and 'should go back where they came from'. It is normal to hold this view and to voice it to others without fear of contradiction.

At school they may be bullies, and may do their best to avoid co-operating, working or sitting with Asian and black classmates – particularly if they can do this without being noticed by their teachers.

They seldom move far from their home and neighbourhood, and in this sense have narrow horizons – they are unfamiliar even with the city where they live, let alone with the countryside or with other countries.

They see racist harassment as a sport or pastime, particularly during the school holidays when there's not much else to do, and when they are travelling between home and school.

Secondary school age range

Offenders are likely to be low achievers, as also probably were their parents, and generally feel that the school does not care about them. In order to achieve a certain self-esteem, to gain respect and prestige in the teenage peer group, they are likely to bully anyone they see as weaker than themselves. If those they pick on are Asian or black, they are likely to justify their behaviour in racist terms.

They engage in continual harassment of local families, particularly if there's a chance of impressing older youths in this way, and are abusive and threatening towards people they pass on the street, particularly those who are strangers in their neighbourhood.

They may well have black or Asian friends at school. But they see no inconsistency between this and their racism. They do not mix with Asian or black people out of school, or after they have left school.

They may engage in physical assaults and violence.

Points for schools

The principal points to emerge from the Home Office research, so far as schools are concerned, is that playground racism must be seen as part of playground culture not just the behaviour of lone individuals; that playground culture is integrally related to street culture; and that street culture, particularly for younger children, is intimately linked to the culture of certain homes and families. This has implications for how incidents of playground racism are dealt with, and for the efforts a school takes to prevent racist incidents occurring in the first place. The researchers identified four possible approaches to offenders, summarised and discussed below.

Ignoring or making light of the incident

Ignoring an incident is seldom if ever appropriate. It permits the offender – and also the offender's friends and associates – to assume that there is nothing wrong with their behaviour and the behaviour may therefore be repeated. Also, this approach gives no support to the pupils who have been attacked. They may consequently assume the teacher and the school generally to be indifferent to racism, and will not bother to complain if there are further incidents.

Rebuke and punishment

This is sometimes entirely appropriate – the offender and any onlookers must be in no doubt that the behaviour is unacceptable, and the pupil who has been attacked must be in no doubt that he or she is supported by the school. But if rebukes and punishments are not complemented by teaching and learning about the reasons why racism is wrong, they may merely feed bitterness and a sense of not being understood. Such bitterness may then be expressed elsewhere, away from the school's awareness.

Reasoning

It is important, certainly, that teachers and youth workers should explain why racism is wrong, and that they should demonstrate with facts and rationality that racist beliefs are both false and harmful. This may involve pointing out that even when a factual statement is true ('They own all the corner shops round here') it does not justify violence or hatred. But like rebukes and punishments, intellectual arguments may merely feed bitterness and a sense of not being understood. If offenders then also feel an increased sense of personal inferiority and powerlessness, and greater resentment of authority, their attitudes and behaviour may become more racist rather than less.

Recognising emotions and anxieties: a holistic approach

Racist beliefs and behaviour in young people have their sources in anxieties about identity and territory, and in desires to belong to a sub-culture of peers or a gang where racism is one (but usually not the only one) of the defining features. Teachers and youth workers should show that they understand such anxieties and desires, and should try to engage with them. A holistic approach involves all pupils, not just those who have engaged in racist behaviour or have made racist remarks, and attention to the curriculum (particularly the citizenship and PSHE curriculum) and to the overall school ethos and atmosphere.

Racism in mainly white schools
findings from research

The most common kind of racist incident in schools is name-calling. It usually takes place in the playground or corridors, or on the streets in the school neighbourhood, not within the earshot of teachers. The offenders are often older and bigger than the people they attack and have an audience of bystanders whose support they take for granted. The view that minority ethnic people 'do not belong here' and 'should go back where they came from' is freely expressed at home by older members of their families. Racist name-calling amongst white children and adolescents is often part of male sub-culture.

Research sponsored by the DfES in mainly white schools in 2001/02 found that 25 per cent of the minority ethnic pupils in the sample had experienced racist name-calling within the previous seven days. Only a tiny proportion of the incidents had been reported to staff. The under-reporting seemed to be connected with a perception amongst many pupils and their parents that staff would be unable or unwilling to take appropriate action.

Source: *Aiming High: understanding the needs of minority ethnic pupils in mainly white schools*, DfES 2004

Frequently asked questions

Why do we have to record and report?

- Schools and LEAs have a statutory duty to report information on racist incidents to the government. This has arisen from the Home Secretary's recommendations following the Stephen Lawrence Inquiry (the Macpherson report.) The purpose of such reporting is to monitor the level of racist incidents nationally and regionally, to look for any patterns in their occurrence and to plan steps to prevent and address them.

- If LEAs feed information back to headteachers and chairs of governors on patterns and trends, they can compare their own experience with aggregated LEA data.

- Procedures of reporting and recording help schools to identify and analyse specific types of incident and therefore contribute to school self-evaluation and action-planning processes. For example, they needs that can be picked up through the PSHE and citizenship curriculum, and through school pastoral processes.

Who will see the information?

- Information from schools should be returned to the LEA in aggregated form. Information submitted by the LEA to the government will be in a statutory aggregated format, showing numbers of incidents and those in which follow-up action has been taken. Individual schools are not named.

Should schools aim for a nil return?

- A school's population does not exist in a vacuum away from the rest of society, nor is it unchanging. It would be unrealistic in any school to expect that racist comments will never be made. A nil return from a school might imply that pupils are not confident about reporting incidents to school staff, or that staff have not understood or not accepted the nature or seriousness of racist incidents.

Will it look bad if a school has a lot of incidents on its return?

- Absolutely not. On the contrary, recording of incidents is evidence that the school has developed a positive atmosphere and ethos in which pupils feel confident that reports will be taken seriously and dealt with.

- If the reporting procedures are successful, an initial increase in the number of incidents reported can be expected, as schools become more successful in promoting this positive ethos. Subsequently it can be expected that the numbers of reported incidents will decrease, as schools develop more effective measures for preventing them.

Do we have to record small, insignificant incidents?

- Yes, every incident, no matter how seemingly small, must be recorded and dealt with. Racist name-calling is hurtful and damaging to the pupil who is attacked and to the school community. If offenders are permitted to believe that racism is acceptable they may become involved later in serious criminal violence.

- Recording seemingly minor incidents can be useful to the school, for example in identifying whether current events or local contexts are causing an increase in harassment of particular pupils.

- It is usually possible to deal with minor incidents straightaway, in the classroom or playground context. Only the more serious or repeated incidents will need reporting on to parents or outside agencies.

If we highlight racist incidents, couldn't this lead to a worse situation?

■ It is certainly important to treat all situations with sensitivity, and therefore to avoid over-reacting or creating martyrs, and in these ways bringing the school rules about racist bullying into disrepute.

■ However, the much more substantial danger lies in ignoring incidents and giving pupils the impression that adults condone racist behaviour. Ignoring incidents means that pupils who are attacked feel unsupported, as do their friends and families, and that offenders feel affirmed and approved of.

How do we decide if an incident is racist?

■ Ofsted has adopted the definition of a racist incident that was created by the Association of Chief Police Officers (ACPO) and modified slightly by the Stephen Lawrence Inquiry report: *'A racist incident is any incident which is perceived to be racist by the victim or any other person.'*

■ A useful working definition in schools is *'behaviour or language that makes a pupil feel unwelcome or marginalised because of their colour, ethnicity, culture, religion or national origin'.*

■ A racist insult may refer to issues of culture or religion as well as to colour and appearance. Anti-Muslim insults and name-calling, for example, should be seen as racist. So should name-calling which targets the Gypsy Traveller community.

■ When an incident perceived to be racist is investigated at a school, the following points should be considered.

   ■ Whether the alleged offender is known to hold racist views or to engage in racist behaviour

   ■ Whether the alleged offender is part of a friendship group known to hold racist views or engage in racist behaviour

   ■ Whether the alleged offender was wearing outward signs of belonging to a racist culture (for example, skinhead clothes and haircut, BNP insignia)

   ■ Whether the clothing of the person attacked clearly identified her or him as belonging to a particular religious or cultural group

   ■ Whether there was no, or only slight, provocation

   ■ Whether there is no other explanation for the incident.

Acknowledgement

The questions and answers on these pages are adapted from *Preventing and Addressing Racism in Schools*, published by Ealing Education Authority in 2003.

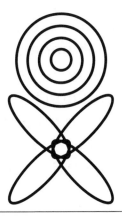

Role-play

The stories on page 71 lend themselves to simple role-played professional conversations. A more elaborate form of role-play involves imagining a staff meeting or governors' meeting, and the provision of role-cards for some of the participants. The four cards here and opposite were prepared for an imaginary governors' meeting at which there was discussion of incorporating into the staff handbook the frequently asked questions that appear on pages 75-76.

At the end of such role-play it is essential that there should be substantial discussion of how people felt, particularly those who took on roles they would not play in real life, and of the principles that have been learnt for dealing with real life.

In such de-briefing and reflection, the material on earlier pages of this chapter will be a useful resource.

Hostile

You consider that there is much too much political correctness around, and that this proposal is a prime example. Children insult each other all the time, they always have and they always will, and calling someone Paki or Gyppo is no worse than calling someone Fatty. The school should be concentrating on the 3Rs, not wasting time with so-called antiracism. You are quick to take offence, particularly if anyone accuses you, or appears to accuse you, of being racist.

Avoidance

Secretly you are against this proposal, for you think it will do more harm than good. The paper smacks of political correctness, and you do not think that so-called racist insults are any worse than other kinds of insult. And anyway, children don't understand what they're saying, they don't mean to be vicious, they just repeat what they have heard their parents say ... However, you don't say any of this at all explicitly. You simply try to divert attention to other matters. You will be successful in this role-play if you can get the group to discuss, preferably in great detail, various red herrings.

Impatient

You are in favour of incorporating this material into the staff handbook. But you want it to be improved, if at all possible. At the very least you want every item to be fully discussed and you want to be confident that each item means the same thing to different people. You are inclined to be impatient with people who don't agree with you and you may well, in this discussion, accuse them of being racist.

Supportive

You are in favour of incorporating this material into the staff handbook. However, it is important in your view that there should be as much consensus as possible. So you try to be supportive not only of the material itself but also of the other members of the group, even if you do not agree with them. Try to get them to change their minds, if you think they are wrong, but do this by showing that you understand where they're coming from. Try not to be confrontational, and to be supportive towards anyone who is distressed or uncomfortable.

Notes on the stories

The following notes show key points likely to arise in discussions of the stories on page 71.

A bit of teasing

Racist name-calling is different from, and more serious than, the other kinds of insult that children and young people trade with each other. The first thing the teacher needs to do here, therefore, is to confirm to the pupil that terms such as 'Paki', even when used in jest or in ignorance, have their history and implications and are totally unacceptable. Also the teacher needs to affirm that the pupil was right to mention the episode – it's not a matter of 'telling tales'- and to show sympathy for the feelings of distress that many South Asian people in Britain feel in connection with international affairs.

It is outrageous, if true, that the class teacher showed little interest. All staff at the school (including administrative and support staff as well as teachers) need to discuss the episode, and other similar episodes. The very process of discussing a story such as this reflectively, and considering various angles on it, is likely to be illuminating. Staff training sessions should therefore contain discussion of such stories. Out of such discussion will come consensus on the unacceptability of racist terms, and on how to explain this to all pupils.

Not fair

Being overweight and being called a Teletubby, or whatever, is not pleasant. On this matter the pupil needs some sympathy and support. The pupil shows some insight into their own behaviour ('I lost it') and this too needs affirming, as does the awareness that terms such as 'Paki' are unacceptable (see above).

Many white people feel a sense of dispossession and dislocation in modern society, and mistakenly attribute this to 'immigrants'. It could be that this feeling is around here, and it may be important therefore to recognise it and talk about it.

It is difficult to tell, since we only have only one side of the story, whether the school indeed acted unfairly.

All insults are hurtful but some are more serious than others, and the school's action may well have been justified. But the pupil's feelings of unfair treatment are also real and could fester into destructive grievance if they are not dealt with.

Not surprising

It's entirely reasonable for a school to insist on certain rules of procedure for classroom discussions, particularly if some of the pupils are likely to be caused distress. Schools need to agree how they will handle issues on which society at large is divided. Such issues include, but are not limited to, issues of immigration and asylum.

Hasn't come to school

This episode is discussed at length in chapter 1.

Get on with your work

Since 9/11 the international situation has frequently had an impact on events in schools and local neighbourhoods in Britain. Schools have to develop consensus amongst staff on how they are going to respond, and how they are going to help pupils to respond. This is not easy, it must be acknowledged.

The lesson sounds rather boring and pointless. The teacher needs guidance not only on how to teach about current affairs, and not only on how to show sensitivity to pupils' concerns and worries, but also on how to plan and run lessons that teach important concepts. For example, on this latter point, the teacher needs to reflect with colleagues on the ideas and points discussed in chapter 2 of this book.

Doesn't seem fair

The headteacher is presumably present at this governors' meeting. He or she has a clear professional duty, if the chair of governors remains silent, to make the simple and time-honoured point that two wrongs do not make a right.

6 PRACTICE INTO POLICY
The letter and spirit of the law

All schools are required by law to write and maintain a formal policy statement on race equality. Broad guidance on what such policies should contain has been issued by the Commission for Racial Equality. The CRE guidance does not, however, refer explicitly to issues of diversity and belonging, and it does not contain detailed guidance on the content of the school curriculum discussed at length here in chapters 2, 3 and 5 of this book, nor on dealing with racist incidents, discussed in chapter 5. This chapter contains the model policy that Derbyshire LEA issued to its schools in early 2001 and subsequently revised slightly. Notes on the policy follow, and suggestions for drawing up action plans.

A model policy

RACE EQUALITY AND CULTURAL DIVERSITY
A MODEL SCHOOL POLICY

Legal duties

1. This school welcomes its duties under the Race Relations Amendment Act 2000, as also the recommendations to schools in the Stephen Lawrence Inquiry report of 1999. Accordingly we are committed to:

- promoting good relations between members of different ethnic, cultural and religious communities, and a common sense of belonging

- preventing and addressing racist behaviour and attitudes

- eliminating unlawful discrimination, and promoting equality of opportunity with a view to achieving equality of outcome

Guiding principles

2. In fulfilling the commitments listed above, we are guided by three essential principles:

Belonging
All pupils should feel that they belong – to the school itself, to our neighbourhood and locality, and to Britain more generally. Belonging involves a shared sense of having a stake in the well-being and future development of the wider community, and a sense that one is accepted and welcomed, and is able and encouraged to participate and contribute. Every pupil should develop the knowledge, understandings and skills they need for taking responsibility to help Britain flourish as a multi-ethnic democracy locally as well as nationally, and within the wider context of an interdependent world.

Identity
Significant differences of culture, outlook, narrative and experience are recognised and respected. Every pupil should be helped to develop a sense of personal and cultural identity that is confident but open to change, and receptive and respectful towards other identities.

Equality
All pupils are of equal value and should have equal opportunities to learn and to be successful. Every pupil should have opportunities to achieve the highest possible standards, and the best possible qualifications for the next stages of their life and education. We are proactive in removing barriers to learning and success.

The curriculum

3. We keep each curriculum subject or area under review in order to ensure that teaching and learning reflect the three principles in paragraph 2 above.

Ethos and organisation

4. We ensure that the principles listed above apply also to the full range of our policies and practices, including those that are concerned with:

- pupils' progress, attainment and assessment

- pupils' personal development and pastoral care

- teaching styles and strategies

- admissions and attendance

- staff recruitment and professional development

- behaviour, discipline and exclusions

- working in partnership with parents and communities.

Addressing racism and xenophobia

5. The school is opposed to all forms of racism and xenophobia, including those forms that are directed towards religious groups and communities, for example antisemitism and Islamophobia, and against Travellers, refugees and asylum-seekers.

6. There is guidance in the staff handbook on how racist incidents should be defined, recorded and dealt with.

7. We take seriously our obligation to report regularly to the LEA about numbers and types of racist incidents at our school and how they were dealt with.

Responsibilities

8. The governing body is responsible for ensuring that the school complies with legislation, and that this policy and its related procedures and strategies are implemented.

9. The headteacher is responsible for implementing the policy; for ensuring that all staff are aware of their responsibilities and are given appropriate training and support; and for taking appropriate action in any cases of unlawful discrimination.

10. All staff are expected to deal with racist incidents that may occur; to know how to identify and challenge racial and cultural bias and stereotyping; to support pupils in their class for whom English is an additional language; and to incorporate principles of equality and diversity into all aspects of their work.

Information and resources

11. We ensure that the content of this policy is known to all staff and governors, and also, as appropriate, to all pupils and parents.

12. All staff and governors have access to a selection of resources which discuss and explain concepts of race equality and cultural diversity in appropriate detail.

Religious observance

13. We respect the religious beliefs and practice of all staff, pupils and parents, and comply with all reasonable requests relating to religious observance and practice.

Action plan

14. We draw up an annual action plan for the implementation of this policy, and for monitoring its impact.

Breaches of the policy

15. Breaches of this policy will be dealt with in the same ways that breaches of other school policies are dealt with, as determined by the headteacher and governing body.

Monitoring and evaluation

16. We collect, study and use quantitative and qualitative data relating to the implementation of this policy, and make adjustments as appropriate.

Date approved by the Governing Body:

Notes on the model policy

1. The model policy on the previous two pages was created in Derbyshire and subsequently slightly expanded and revised. It was published in 2001 by the journal *Multicultural Teaching* in association with Uniting Britain Trust and appeared on several websites. Versions of it were used by several other LEAs besides Derbyshire and by many individual schools throughout Britain.

2. Under the Race Relations (Amendment) Act, every school in Britain is required to prepare and maintain a such a policy. It may be a freestanding paper or else may be part of a wider policy, for example on equal opportunities generally. If part of a wider policy, the race equality component must be easily identifiable.

3. The model policy statement on the previous two pages was compiled in accordance with the *Code of Practice on the Duty to Promote Race Equality* issued by the Commission for Racial Equality in December 2001, and *Preparing a Race Equality Policy for Schools*, issued in March 2002. The CRE's handbook *Learning for All* is also a helpful guide. There is full information about these publications on the CRE's website at www.cre.gov.uk.

4. In addition, the model policy statement reflects concerns and concepts in *The Future of Multi-Ethnic Britain*, 2000; *The Stephen Lawrence Inquiry*,1999; and *Guidance on Community Cohesion*, published by the Local Government Association in 2002. The philosophical argument in these reports is that the promotion of race equality necessarily involves also the recognition of cultural diversity and the development of social cohesion. The principles of diversity and cohesion need to be explicitly mentioned, for otherwise they may be neglected.

5. Further, the draft statement is consistent with the requirements and expectations of Ofsted, as presented in *Evaluating Educational Inclusion: guidance for inspectors and schools*, issued in 2000, and *Raising the Attainment of Minority Ethnic Pupils: school and LEA responses*, issued in 1999. The duties of Ofsted when inspecting schools with specific regard to the Race Relations (Amendment) Act are set out in *A Framework for Inspectorates*, published by the Commission for Racial Equality.

6. What a policy statement actually says matters a great deal. That is why many local authorities have issued a model statement for schools to adopt or to modify. Also, however, processes of discussion and deliberation are of great importance, as are processes of keeping a policy under review, and the arrangements and action plans that are made to implement it. The crucial importance of careful deliberation involving all staff is well illustrated here on later pages in the case-study from one school.

7. It is valuable if a senior member of staff at each school is designated to lead on the development of the policy, and that he or she should establish appropriate procedures for consulting and involving others, both within the school and outside. The same person could be responsible for ensuring that the policy is kept under review and that its impact is evaluated, and for co-ordinating the school's action plan to implement it. In many schools it is also valuable if a member of the governing body has lead responsibility for keeping the policy under review, as shown in the case-study here on later pages. The case study also underlines the importance of having a school coordinator for multicultural education.

8. The headings in the model statement are recommended, not statutory. There are further notes on them below.

Legal duties

It is useful to start a policy by recalling the legal obligation. The form of words in the model statement expands slightly on the words in the Race Relations Act, in order to emphasise the importance not only of race equality but also of identity and belonging.

Guiding principles

The three principles stated here are discussed at length in the 2000 report of the Commission on the Future of Multi-Ethnic Britain.

Curriculum

This is such an important component of school life that it merits a special mention. Chapters 2, 3 and 4 of this handbook are about the potential of each curriculum subject or area to promote learning about cultural diversity and race equality.

Ethos and organisation

The list in the model statement is based on CRE guidance. Schools can of course add to it or re-order it if they wish.

Addressing racism and xenophobia

There is a legal requirement, following the Stephen Lawrence Inquiry report, that LEAs should collect information from all schools each year about racist incidents and that Ofsted should inspect compliance. It is appropriate, therefore, that a school race equality policy should contain an explicit commitment to opposing racist behaviour. The wording in the model adds the term 'xenophobia' to reflect European usage, and to refer to the full range of issues requiring attention.

Responsibilities

The CRE recommends that the responsibilities of governors, headteachers and other staff should be explicitly stated, as in the model statement.

Information and resources

There is a legal obligation that policy statements should be publicly available, and that staff should be supported by resources and training. The case-study on later pages refers to the value of a central resources list issued to all staff.

Religious observance

A reference to religious observance is not obligatory under the Race Relations Act. However, it is appropriate to include reference to this topic in a policy statement on race equality and cultural diversity. Reasonable adjustment in employment issues for religious observance has been obligatory throughout the European Union since December 2003.

Action plan

The CRE stresses that statements of policy should be linked to an action plan. On later pages here there is a list of items that might be included in such a plan. Of course, not all the items in the list are equally relevant or urgent in all schools.

Evaluation and monitoring

There must be a commitment to collecting and using data. The data must include, but need not be limited to, statistical information about attainment and pupils' experiences.

Breaches of the policy

The CRE recommends that there should be a statement in writing about what steps will be taken if there are breaches of the policy. The Derbyshire model suggests that it is sufficient to indicate that the same procedures will be adopted as for any other breach of school policy.

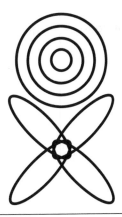

Points for an Action Plan

Some of the following points could be included in a school action plan. Not all the points are equally relevant or urgent in all schools.

School improvement plan

1. Ensure that there are references to race equality and cultural diversity issues in the school development plan.

Continuing professional development

2. Ensure that there are references to race equality and cultural diversity issues in the school's programmes and plans for induction and staff training, both of teaching staff and support staff, and also for the governing body.

3. Consider the methods and content of staff training on race equality and cultural diversity issues, and how such training is appropriately evaluated.

Statement about the school's composition and context

4. Draw up a statement about the composition of the school by ethnicity, home language and religion, and about the nature of the neighbourhood(s) the school serves.

5. Refer to the climate of opinion in the school and in the neighbourhood on issues relating to race equality and cultural diversity, and to the school's priorities over the next 12 months.

Auditing and review

6. Assess the impact of current policies through consultation, evaluation and auditing tools, for example the Commission for Racial Equality's *Learning for All* or those which appear in chapter 4 of *Here, There and Everywhere*.

7. Ensure that the results of auditing are reported to the governing body and made available, as appropriate, to other interested parties.

Monitoring of results

8. Review our procedures for monitoring attainment by ethnicity and gender, and how we use the results of such monitoring.

9. Use data on attainment, broken down by both ethnicity and gender, to review the school's progress over time and in comparison with other schools, and to identify areas for improvement and development.

10. Fulfil the duties schools have to take reasonable steps to make available annually the results of such assessments and monitoring.

Attainment, progress and assessment

11. Review ways in which we ensure that we have and communicate high expectations of all pupils

12. Consider how we recognise and value a wide range of achievement.

13. Take action to reduce and remove disparities between pupils from different communities and backgrounds.

Curriculum content

14. In each subject, and in the curriculum as a whole, ensure opportunities are taken to teach about race equality and cultural diversity.

15. Use in this connection the auditing forms in chapter 4 in *Here, There and Everywhere*.

16. Consider in particular the areas of the curriculum where pupils explore concepts and issues relating to identity, racial justice and racism; global interdependence; and shared humanity.

17. Review how we ensure that learning about cultural diversity includes personal encounter with other cultures.

18. Review how extra-curricular activities and events cater for the interests and capabilities of all pupils, and take account of parental concerns related to religion and culture.

Personal development and pastoral care

19. Ensure that pastoral support takes account of religious and cultural concerns and of the experiences and needs of particular groups of pupils, for example Gypsy/Roma, Travellers of Irish heritage, refugees and asylum seekers.

20. Encourage all students to consider a wide range of career and post-16 options.

21. Monitor work experience opportunities by ethnicity to ensure that there is no stereotyping in placements and to check whether students encounter racism in the workplaces to which they are attached.

22. Consider how the school supports people affected by racist attacks, abuse and harassment, whether in the school or the neighbourhood.

Partnerships with parents and communities

23. Encourage the involvement and participation of all parents in the school.

24. Ensure that information and material for parents is accessible in user-friendly language, and in languages and formats other than English, as appropriate.

25. Ensure that premises and facilities are fully accessible to and used by a wide range of local groups and communities.

Racism, racial harassment and school ethos

26. Review procedures for recording, investigating and reporting incidents of racism, and for supporting those who are targeted or attacked and dealing with offenders.

27. Provide training, guidance and support for staff, including administrative staff, to ensure that they can all deal firmly, consistently and effectively with racist incidents and bullying.

28. Ensure that pupils, parents and staff are aware of the procedures for dealing with racist incidents and harassment.

29. Work with the local authority and other partners to tackle racist behaviour, abuse and harassment within the local area.

Staff recruitment and professional development

30. Review arrangements for ensuring that good equal opportunities practice operates throughout the selection and recruitment process.

31. Monitor and report on the composition of the staff by ethnicity, gender and seniority or grade.

32. Monitor by ethnicity and gender all applications for employment, training and promotion.

Admissions and attendance

33. Ensure the admissions criteria are equally open to pupils from all communities.

34. Monitor the admissions process to ensure it is administered consistently and fairly to pupils from all backgrounds and communities.

35. Monitor pupil attendance by ethnicity and community background.

Case-study from one school

This page outlines the process of policy-making in one Derbyshire school. It illustrates the importance of careful and sustained deliberation, and the need for policy to be owned by all teaching and support staff and by the governing body.

1. Attendance at LEA event (March and June 2001)
The head and deputy head attend sessions run by the LEA about the Stephen Lawrence Inquiry report. A presentation by the theatre-in-education company Actorshop, specially commissioned by Derbyshire, makes a great impression on them. (For further information about the show, see chapter 1.) They decide that they must definitely review and improve the school umprovement plan.

2. Inset session for all staff – A (October 2001)
A twilight session is held for all staff, including clerical and administrative staff, mid-day supervisors and teaching assistants. Staff from neighbouring schools are also invited. The previous evening the Actorshop company has presented the show it originally developed for the LEA (see above). There is animated and enthusiastic discussion of the drama and strong feeling that the school community as a whole should move towards a common understanding of the nature of racism and of the urgent importance of tacking it in its various forms.

3. Inset session for all staff – B (October 2001)
The following week there is again a twilight session for all staff. All governors are also invited. The purpose is to work towards shared understanding of acceptable vocabulary and behaviour, and to begin reviewing all aspects of the school's curriculum and ethos with regard to race equality and cultural diversity issues. All staff fill in evaluation forms and there is agreement that these will be revisited later in the year. On the same day there is a workshop for mid-day supervisors on the definition of racist incidents and on ways of dealing with them.

4. Agenda item at meetings (from November 2001)
Antiracism and multiculturalism are to be standard items on the agenda of staff meetings for the rest of the year. Subject co-ordinators are given copies of a paper to help them audit and review their curriculum area and to plan developments and improvements. (A much expanded version of the paper is provided in this handbook.) It is agreed that a report on racist incidents will be a routine agenda item at all governor meetings.

5. Lesson planning proformas (from November 2001)
The school's proformas for lesson planning and evaluation are modified to incorporate an explicit requirement to consider issues of cultural diversity.

6. Link governor appointed (January 2002)
A link governor is appointed to have oversight of issues relating to cultural diversity and race equality.

7. Draft policy statement (March 2002)
In preparation for the legal requirement that every school should have a formal statement of policy, a draft is prepared for discussion with all staff, parents and governors.

8. Agreed statement in school prospectuses (April 2002)
All headteachers in the town agree a common statement for inclusion in school prospectuses, stressing their commitment to promoting multicultural education and dealing with racist incidents.

9. Audit and cataloguing of resources (April/May 2002)
The school's coordinator for multicultural education draws up an extensive list of resources and materials held at the school and this is distributed to all staff.

10. Review of the year (July 2002)
The evaluation forms filled in last October are revisited and progress is reviewed.

11. Inset day at the Rainbow Centre (October 2002)
All staff attend a training day at the Rainbow Centre, Derby, and all governors are invited.

Source: Long Row Primary School, Belper, Derbyshire.

7 RESOURCES
references, websites, bibliography, addresses

In the first section of this chapter there are notes and acknowledgements relating to the main text. They indicate the sources of ideas and make suggestions for further reading. The second section is a substantial guide to useful websites. For convenience, an updated copy of this is available on the internet; you can find it at www.insted.co.uk /links.html. The third section gives bibliographical details for all the works cited in the *Views and voices* boxes in chapters 2 and 3, and for all those mentioned in the references.

References

Page

1   The website is at www.here-there-everywhere. com. It contains information about the project's design and activities; the schools, students and pupils who are involved in it; and the Barclays New Futures scheme that funds it.

2   The forum theatre presentation was by Actorshop, Cedar Court, 47 Memorial Avenue, London E15 3BT. Tel: 020 7511 1197, email: training@actorshop.demon.co.uk. There is further reference to *Sticks, Stones and Macpherson* on page 88. Another fine piece of forum theatre worth mentioning is *Ally Comes to Cumbria*, developed by Global Link (www. globallink.org.uk) for Cumbria LEA.

7   An earlier and much briefer version of chapter 2 appears in the DfES publication *Aiming High: understanding the needs of minority ethnic pupils in mainly white schools* (2004) and is reflected in East Sussex County Council's *Developing Excellence in Race Equality in our Schools* (2004).

8   The five aims of humanities teaching are from Bruner (1967). They are adapted slightly here, to make the language inclusive.

12 Many valuable materials on globalisation have been developed over the years by the Tide Centre, Birmingham. They include *Globalisation – what's it all about*, referred to in the classroom examples on page 31. The centre's postal and website addresses are in the list at the end of the bibliography.

18 For discussion of Islamophobia as a form of racism see the 2004 report of the Commission on British Muslims and Islamophobia. There is an extract entitled *Islamophobia and race relations* at www.insted.co.uk/islam.html

21 The discussions and examples in chapter 3 are derived from a range of sources, including Cambridgeshire County Council (2002), Qualifications and Curriculum Authority (2003), Runnymede Trust (1993, 2003) and the School Development Support Agency (2004). Full details are in the bibliography. Particular acknowledgment is due to the School Development Support Agency.

22 The quotation from Keats is from a letter dated 21 December 1817. The concept of negative capability is referred to throughout Philip Pullman's trilogy, *His Dark Materials*. There is a brief extract from the final pages of the trilogy on page 42.

37 The quotation from Munir Fasheh's influential lecture has been slightly edited so that it accords with UK rather than US English. The full text of the lecture can be found easily through a Google search on the internet.

38 Anowara Jehaan's translation of Tagore's poem *Bangla Beshai* was cited in an article by Chris Searle (1985).

39 Some of the classroom activities on this page, including the one about a visit to a francophone country, are adapted from the QCA's *Respect for All* website.

41 Most of the classroom activities on this page are adapted from guidelines published by Cambridgeshire Multicultural Education Service, 2002.

42 The references in *Views and voices 53* are to great West Indian cricketers of an earlier generation: Sir Gary Sobers, Everton Weekes, Frank Worrell and Clyde Walcott.

43 There is further information about persona dolls in Brown (2001) and Bowles (2004) and there are vivid case studies about their use in *Celebrating Diversity* produced by Team Video in association with Personal Doll training (2004).

69 There is substantial material about bullying at www.dfes.gov.uk/bullying. The material is suitable for both pupils and teachers and some of it is in a range of community languages.

76 The Home Office research was conducted by Rae Sibbitt. Full details are in the list of works cited on pages 97-98.

Websites

Please note: an updated version of this list is available at www.insted.co.uk. It contains hyperlinks to all the sites mentioned and is therefore more convenient to use than this printed list. All addresses here were correct as of August 2004.

Sites providing general information

The principal sources of information on race and ethnicity issues in the UK include the following. Several have extensive links to other sites.

Commission for Racial Equality (www.cre.gov.uk)
Substantial information about the Race Relations (Amendment) Act. Materials include a quiz with comments and notes on the correct answers.

The Guardian Newspaper (www.guardian.co.uk/race)
There is a special section archiving all articles and reports about race equality since 1998. An excellent resource.

Institute of Race Relations (www.irr.org.uk)
Amongst other things, IRR sends out a weekly newsletter about current events. Well worth subscribing.

Home Office (www.homeoffice.gov.uk – click then on Community and race)
The lead government department concerned with race equality issues.

Muslim Council of Britain (www.mcb.org.uk)
Extensive information, and with many links to other Muslim sites.

1990 Trust (www.blink.org.uk)
Large collection of recent newspaper articles and reports, helpfully catalogued, giving a comprehensive picture of the current scene.

General guidance for schools

The DfES Ethnic Minority Achievement site (http://www.standards.dfes.gov.uk/ethnicminorities) has a wide range of guidance and information and many links to other government sites.

A valuable one-stop-shop has been set up by Portsmouth EMAS providing links to all the principal government documents and reports of recent years. Go to http://www.blss.portsmouth.sch.uk/default.htm and then in the quick search facility (top right hand corner) click on Advice – recent key documents.

Multiverse, funded by the Teacher Training Agency, has a valuable archive of academic articles about race equality in education and many materials for continuing professional development ((www.multiverse.ac.uk).

The EMA Online site for ethnic minority achievement (www.emaonline.org.uk) is a resource base for teachers developed by Birmingham, Leeds and Manchester LEAs with funding from the DfES. It contains many practical ideas and links.

There is substantial information and guidance relating to the Race Relations (Amendment) Act at www.cre.gov.uk. Click on Good practice on the home page and then on Education in the list entitled Sectors. For case study examples of race equality policies and programmes in mainly white schools it is worth visiting www.warwickshire.gov.uk/raceequality.

QCA has developed a website to support the education of new arrivals from overseas. There is information on educational and welfare rights and background information concerning many countries of origin.

The Centre for Education for Race Equality in Scotland (www.education.ed.ac.uk/ceres) has a wealth of advice and information about good practice and whole-school policy.

Warwickshire Education Department has a wide range of resources, ideas and advice for schools. Developed in just one local authority but with relevance everywhere.

Teacher World (www.teacherworld.co.uk), based at Leeds Metropolitan University and funded by the Teacher Training Agency, has a particular focus on the experiences and perceptions of Asian and black teachers.

The Respect for All website of the Qualifications and Curriculum Authority has a substantial range of practical suggestions and guidelines for incorporating multicultural perspectives in all curriculum subjects. Go to gca.org.uk, then Ages 3-14, then Inclusion, then Respect for All.

Legal requirements

There is substantial information and guidance relating to the Race Relations (Amendment) Act at www.cre.gov.uk. Click on Good practice on the home page and then on Education in the list entitled Sectors.

The inspection regimes throughout Britain are legally required to inspect the ways in which schools implement policies on race equality and cultural diversity. In this connection it is valuable to study the criteria Ofsted uses, as set out in *Evaluating Educational Inclusion: guidance for inspectors and schools*, issued in 2000. This can be downloaded from the Ofsted website at www.ofsted.gov.uk. There is also a comprehensive list of relevant Ofsted documents on the Portsmouth LEA site.

In April 2002 Ofsted published two reports about good practice in the education of African-Caribbean pupils. Both can be downloaded in PDF format from Ofsted's website.

Also on the Ofsted website is its race equality scheme, dated June 2002. Amongst other things, this acknowledges Ofsted's 'important role in checking the compliance of bodies under inspection with the legal duties that relate to them and commenting on the effectiveness of their plans'.

Culture and identity

There is clear and useful information about cultural diversity in Britain at www.bbc.co.uk/londonlive. Click on the icon for United Colours of London. Basic facts are provided about ten separate communities: Bangladeshi, Caribbean, Chinese, Ethiopian, Greek, Indian, Irish, Pakistani, Turkish and West African. The focus is on London, but most of the information is relevant for the whole of Britain.

The BBC has valuable sites on black history for school pupils at www.bbc.co.uk/education/archive/histfile/mystery.htm and, with particular reference to its excellent Windrush series, www.bbc.co.uk/education/archive/windrush.

The Britkid site, funded by Comic Relief, is well worth visiting. Lively and enjoyable, it is intended in the first instance for primary school pupils in areas where there are few people of African, Asian or Caribbean background. But its interest is in fact much wider. It was updated in 2002 and is well worth visiting for valuable ideas and insights. The address is www.britkid.org/

Based on the Britkid concept, there is an anti-bullying site entitled www.coastkid.org. It focuses on the relationships, behaviours and conflicts that arise between nine young people in an imaginary school on the south coast.

The Blacknet site is lively and interactive, and contains an eclectic and fascinating collection of materials, including not only much of historical interest and but also valuable information about the present. Its address is www.blacknet.co.uk. There are extensive links to other relevant sites.

Similarly there is a wealth of information about black communities in Britain at www.everygeneration.co.uk, the winner of the website category in the 2003 Race in the Media (RIMA) awards scheme run by the Commission for Racial Equality.

For information about Islam and British Muslims, visit the IQRA Trust at www.iqratrust.org.uk. In August 2003 the Muslim Council of Britain (www.mcb.org.uk) set up an excellent and comprehensive portal about Islam and this is now an invaluable place to start enquiries.

The Muslim Heritage site (www.muslimheritage.com) has excellent materials on the history of Islamic civilisation, concentrating in particular on developments in science and technology.

At the website of the Muslim Home School Network, based in the United States (www.muslimhomeschool.com/pride/edmaterial/Sharing.htm) there is the fascinating Spread of Knowledge game, illustrating science as a universal human activity.

There is a substantial list of sites dealing with Islamic culture at www.insted.co.uk/websites.html.

The Indobrit (www.indobrit.com) site has been set up to discuss issues of interest to the younger generation of British people who are of Indian, particularly Gujarati, heritage.

Youthweb, developed by Soft Touch Community Arts, is a lively site for secondary students, and for teachers and youth workers. The materials on racism and identity have been created by young people in Leicester. On the home page click on the 'Respect' button. The site is at www.youth-web.org.uk.

Racism and Islamophobia

The whole of the Stephen Lawrence Inquiry report is at http://www.official-documents.co.uk/document/cm42/4262/sli-06.htm. The section dealing with institutional racism is Chapter 6 and is well worth downloading, printing and studying. There is also much valuable material about the Stephen Lawrence Inquiry on the *Guardian* site, www.guardian.co.uk/race, and the site of the 1990 Trust, www.blink.org.uk.

The Ofsted (www.ofsted.gov.uk.) document *Evaluating Educational Inclusion: guidance for inspectors and schools*, contains a useful four-page annex entitled 'Issues for Inspection arising from the Macpherson Report'. This quotes and explains the recommendations in the report that apply to schools, and refers also to the valuable Ofsted report issued in 1999, *Raising the Attainment of Minority Ethnic Pupils: school and LEA responses.*

An impressive LEA project in response to the report is an awards scheme for schools set up by Leeds. Full details at www.leedslearning.net/lawrence.

Campaigns against racism in and around football grounds are a significant development in recent years. Much valuable information is available from the Football Unites Racism Divides project (FURD) set up by Sheffield United, www.furd.org. The national Show Racism the Red Card campaign is at www.srtrc.org.

With regard to campaigns on other topics, there is valuable information at the website of the Campaign Against Racism and Fascism, www.carf.demon.co.uk.

There is substantial coverage of racism at the site of the Institute of Race Relations. One of the Institute's valuable services is the provision of a weekly newsletter principally about events reported in local newspapers.

There are extracts from the 2004 report of the Commission on British Muslims and Islamophobia, including a paper entitled *Islamophobia and Race Relations*, at www.insted.co.uk/islam.html.

The National Association of Schoolmasters and Women Teachers has compiled a useful booklet on Islamophobia. It's available at their website (www.nasuwt.org.uk) and also in print. It contains several useful guidelines for teaching about Islam and Islamophobia and reprints advice to schools issued by the Government after 9/11.

The Insted consultancy has published workshop papers on dealing with racist incidents in schools at www.insted.co.uk/race.html.

Teaching about controversial issues

Many organisations have issued sets of guidelines over the years. One of the best is *Teaching on Controversial Issues: guidelines for teachers* by Alan Shapiro, writing for Educators for Social Responsibility (ESR) Metropolitan Area, United States. The address is www.esrmetro.org/teaching controversy.html. A controversial issue, Shapiro recalls, is one on which there are conflicting definitions, facts, assumptions, opinions and solutions, competing feelings and values, and public debates and disagreements.

The national ESR office published a substantial document entitled *Talking to Children about War and Violence in the World*. It can be downloaded from www.esrnational.org. The purpose is to help adults think about the impact of war on young people, understand how children's needs differ at various ages, and choose appropriate responses.

Other useful papers about controversial issues include *Tips for Teaching Controversial Issues* at www.streetlaw.org/controversy2.html, a paper about Iraq issued by the Citizenship Foundation at www.citizenshipfoundation.org.uk and a brief statement by the Qualifications and Curriculum Agency at www.qca.org.uk/ca.inclusion/respect_for_all. The headings in the latter are 'use appropriate resources', 'provide a broad and balanced view of cultures', 'challenge assumptions', 'understand globalisation' and 'create an open climate'.

The Muslim Home School Network, based in the United States, www.muslimhomeschool.com provides a substantial and extremely valuable list of resources and articles for teaching and talking about 9/11.

The BBC Newsround site (www.bbc.co.uk/cbbcnews) provides lesson plans. At the time of the Iraq conflict they included *Reporting on Conflict – why do we say truth is the first casualty of war?*; *Kids' Anti-War Marches – the strengths and weaknesses of non-violent conflict resolution*; and *Iraq Briefing – a briefing document for journalists reporting the war*. There was also a simple quiz as a warm-up activity and there were several briefing papers written for the 8-14 age-group.

The Rethinking Schools website, based in the United States, has a wide range of materials for teachers about the current international situation. There are maps, statistics, notes on history, suggestions for poetry and songs, facts about Islam and about Arab culture and civilisation, definitions and discussions of terrorism, details of anti-war campaigns, resource lists and several lesson plans. The overall orientation is clearly against the American government's current policies. The address is www.rethinkingschools. org/war.

The National Union of Teachers provided clear and comprehensive guidance entitled *War in Iraq – the impact on schools*. It is available as a PDF document and also as a Word document so that you can re-format and customise it, if you wish, for your own school. It can be found through www.teachers.org.uk.

There is a wealth of material at www.re-xs.ucsm.ac. uk, run by St Martin's College, Lancaster. The website is intended primarily for teachers of religious education. But it contains many items of general interest, and much that is valuable for the planning of school assemblies. There are links to a wide range of other sites, mainly in the UK, and copies of important statements about the international situation issued by faith communities in Britain, both locally and nationally.

Also the Culham Institute prepared materials for school assemblies and is well worth visiting at www.culham.ac.uk. The titles include *The Dove of Hope, Friends not Enemies*, and *Never Alone*. There are also suggestions for prayers, hymns and songs, and in an essay entitled *Primary Schools and Images of War* there are some useful guidelines for planning collective worship.

Judith Myers-Walls, a child development specialist based at Purdue University, Indiana, published *When War is in the News* in February 2003 at www.ces. purdue.edu/terrorism. There are also several other useful papers at this site, intended in particular for teachers and parents of the very young.

The American Psychological Association has a wide range of checklists and papers for parents and teachers, including 'Ten Steps for Resilience in Time of War'. The address is http://helping.apa.org/resilience.

Refugees and people seeking asylum

For a wide range of information and resources on refugees and asylum-seekers, visit the Refugee Council, www.refugeecouncil.org.uk.

Specifically on educational matters, and for much useful advice and guidance, go to www.refugee education.co.uk.

Practical and authoritative advice from the government can be downloaded from www. teachernet.gov.uk/mailingBank/EducatAsylum Seeking.pdf

The Praxis site (www.praxis.org.uk) has much useful material about media treatment of asylum and refugee issues, and also a number of stories by refugees to Britain recounting their experiences.

For valuable ideas, resources and links about Refugee Week, celebrated each June, go to www.refugeeweek. org.uk.

For World Refugee Day, there are ideas and resources at www.worldrefugeeday.info/

There are resources relating to recent events, including a set of material and full-text documents concerning UK proposals for transit processing centres and regional protection zones at www. asylumrights.net

There is a valuable discussion group for teachers, with information about new resources and events, at refed-subscribe@yahoogroups.com. To subscribe, simply send an empty message.

The National Coalition of Anti-Deportation Campaigns provides much useful information about legal matters, and stories about individuals and families. The website is at www.ncadc.org.uk.

On opposition to the government's segregation policies and proposals it's worth visiting www. segregation.org.uk.

The Institute for Race Relations has published articles and papers about what it calls 'xeno-racism', and these have a European as well as a British dimension. Details at http://www.irr.org.uk/

English as an additional language

Several local authorities have published valuable guidance on supporting bilingual pupils in the mainstream classroom. They include Hampshire, Hounslow (www.ealinhounslow.org.uk), Manchester (www.manchester.gov.uk/education/emas) and Portsmouth (http://www.blss.portsmouth.sch.uk/default.htm)

A wealth of practical teaching ideas can be found at the Collaborative Learning Project (www.collaborativelearning.org), City of Nottingham (www.nottinghamschools.co.uk – click then on Standards and Effectiveness, followed by EMAG) and the Gordon Ward Consultancy (http://homepage.ntlworld.com/gordon.ward2000/)

At the home-school-community pages on the Portsmouth site (http://www.blss.portsmouth.sch.uk/hsc/index.shtml) there is valuable information about a range of languages other than English and about the distinctive difficulties that speakers of them may have when learning English. There is a link to the Houghton Mifflin English Language Centre in the United States, where similar information is available about several further languages.

The British Educational Communications and Technology Agency (BECTA) has published *Using ICT to Support EAL* by Sheilagh Crowther, a member of Gloucestershire's Ethnic Minorities Achievement Service. The document is a wide-ranging and easy-to-read guide to ways of using ICT with pupils for whom English is an additional language. BECTA has also produced sheets which translate common ICT terms and computer-related phrases from English into other languages, and some sheets about science apparatus, hazards and safety. On the homepage (www.becta.org.uk) write ESOL Resources in the search facility.

Another source of key words in other languages is the Refugee Council. It publishes a valuable series of books with the generic title of *Words for School Life*. Key words are provided in Albanian, Arabic, Bosnian, Kurdish Sorani, Kurdish Turkish, Persian and Somali.

The English Club site (http://games.english club.com/) has a wide range of games for children and adults learning English as an additional language. Many of the games are suitable for native speakers of English also.

The National Primary and Key Stage 3 strategies have produced considerable guidance for teaching pupils learning English as an additional language. Primary guidance can be found at http://www.standards.dfes.gov.uk/literacy/communities/inclusion/?leaf=2

To access Key Stage 3 guidance and online publications, go to http://www.standards.dfes.gov.uk/keystage3 and search using keyword Targeted Support – EAL (English as an Additional Language).

Clicker 4 is a frequently used ICT tool to support EAL learners and there is a collection of case studies at http://www.cricksoft.com/uk/ideas/case_studies/index.htm Free grids can be downloaded from the Clicker Grids for Learning website http://www.learninggrids.com/ Coventry LEA has identified sets of grids that are particularly useful for EAL learners. Details can be obtained from MGSS, Prior Deram Walk, Coventry CV4 8FT, telephone 02476 717800.

The National Association for Language Development in the Curriculum (NALDIC) provides advice on a range of policy and practice matters relating to English as an additional language at www.naldic.org.uk.. A particularly useful new section of the website contains online readings for initial teacher educators which address many of the basic questions about learning EAL. The address is www.naldic.org.uk/ittseal/research/readings.cfm

The Northern Association of Support Services concerned with language and bilingualism (NASSEA) has a website at www.nassea.org.uk. There are details here about conferences and courses in northern England, and links to downloadable documents produced in northern LEAs.

It is well worth joining the EAL-BILINGUAL mailing list. Teachers of EAL throughout Britain use it to share information, ideas and queries, all closely related to practice. To join the list, send an email to majordomo@ngfl.gov.uk. Make sure to leave the space for 'Subject' blank. In the body of the message simply write the following words: *subscribe eal-bilingual.*

For an extensive range of academic and practical papers about bilingual education in the United States visit the excellent Rethinking Schools site (www.rethinkingschools.org)

Links with schools in other countries

The British Council in Australia has set up the Montage Internet project to help schools make links with schools in other countries. The website is intended for pupils as well as teachers. Specific projects include Celebrations and Commemorations, Travel Buddies, Human Rights, The Common Good, Oceans Alive (on biodiversity) and Kids on the Net. The address is www.britishcouncil.org.au/montage.

It is in addition valuable to join the Montageplus project, similarly designed and run by the British Council in Australia. Membership is free of charge and members receive regular email mailings. The address is www.montageplus.co.uk

The Central Bureau for International Education and Training is at www.centralbureau.org.uk and Windows on the World provides assistance with finding partners in other countries. Its address is www.wotw.org.uk.

The Department for International Development funds a programme to encourage global awareness in UK schools through links with schools in Africa, Asia, Latin America and the Caribbean. It's at www.wotw.org.uk/northsouth. Amongst other things, it contains information about the financial resources that are available as grants. Such information can also be obtained by emailing to world.links@british council.org.

Citizenship Education

For curriculum materials on citizenship education more generally, particularly with regard to Key Stages 3 and 4, go to the Centre for Citizenship Studies in Education at the University of Leicester. There is a wealth here of valuable ideas and advice, and information about resources and other sites. The address is www.citizenship-global.org.uk.

There is information about government policy, expectations and requirements at www.dfes.gov.uk/citizenship. It's also worth visiting the Hansard Society at www.hansardsociety.org.uk; the lesson plans at www.learn.co.uk/citizenship; and the Association of Citizenship Teaching at www.teachingcitizenship.org.uk.

For resources on a world dimension in the curriculum, the Development Education Centre in Birmingham has a wealth of useful information and materials. The address is www.tidec.org.uk.

Further sources of materials about world affairs include the Development Education Despatch Unit at www.dedu.gn.apc.org, Save the Children at www.savethechildren.org.uk, Oxfam at www.oxfam.org.uk/coolplanet, and Worldwide Fund for Nature at www.wwf-uk.org.

European dimensions

The European Monitoring Centre on Racism and Xenophobia (EUMC), based in Vienna, is establishing a sound reputation as a provider of reliable information. Its website is at http://eumc.eu.int.

The European Commission against Racism and Intolerance, based in Strasbourg, is an activity of the Council of Europe. It has representatives from 43 different countries. The website is at www.coe.int.

The European Multicultural Foundation and Minorities of Europe are based in London and Coventry respectively. Their sites are at www.em-foundation.org.uk and www.moe-online.com.

Suppliers, booksellers and publishers

Educational books, dolls, puppets, puzzles and posters can be ordered through www.positive-identity.com. It is also well worth visiting Multicultural Books, formerly Paublo Books, at www.multiculturalbooks.co.uk They have over 6000 titles and Blossom Jackson (blossom@multiculturalbooks.demon.co,uk) is pleased to respond to enquiries from teachers and to give advice.

The Willesden Bookshop has lists of multicultural collections (including many valuable materials imported from the United States) at www.willesden bookshop.co.uk.

Letterbox Library has an extensive list entitled 'Celebrating Equality and Diversity in the Best Children's Books'. Its website is at www.letterbox library.com.

The principal publishing house specialising in race and diversity issues for educational practitioners is Trentham Books. Their catalogue is at www.trentham-books.co.uk.

Bromley Centre for Multicultural Resources has an extensive selection of artefacts, books and videos and has catalogued them on its website, together with a helpful search facility.

List of works cited

(An asterisk indicates that the publication is more easily obtained from an organisation than a bookseller. The addresses of all organisations cited are given at the end.)

Ahmed, Rehana ed (2004) *Walking a Tightrope: new writing from Asian Britain*, London: Young Picador

Angelou, Maya (1998) *Even the Stars Look Lonesome*, London: Virago

Beddis, Rex (1983) Geographical Education since 1960: a personal view, in John Huckle, ed, *Geographical Education: reflection and action*, Oxford University Press

Behlic, Zafir (2003) I Am What I Choose To Be, *In Exile*, London: Refugee Council

Bennett, Arnold (1910) *Clayhanger*, re-issued in 1975 by Penguin Books

Birmingham Advisory Support Service (2002) We Also Served, Birmingham: BASS*

Bowles, Marilyn (2004) *The Little Book of Persona Dolls*, Lutterworth: Featherstone Publications

Brown, Babette (2001) *Combating Discrimination: Persona dolls in action*, Stoke on Trent: Trentham Books

Bruner, Jerome (1967) *Toward a Theory of Instruction*, Harvard University Press

Burgess, Anthony (1980) *Earthly Powers*, London: Hutchinson

Cambridgeshire Multicultural Education Service (2002) *Valuing Cultural Diversity: curriculum guidance*, Cambridgeshire County Council

Centre for World Development Education (1980) *Change and Choice: Britain in an interdependent world*, London: CWDE

Churches' Commission for Racial Justice (2003) *Redeeming the Time: all God's people must challenge racism*, London: Churches Together in Britain and Ireland

Cockcroft, John (1982) *Mathematics Counts*, London: Department for Education and Science

Commission on British Muslims and Islamophobia (2004) *Islamophobia: issues, challenges and action*, Stoke on Trent: Trentham Books

Commission on Multi-Ethnic Britain (2000) *The Future of Multi-Ethnic Britain*, London: Profile Books

Churches Commission for Racial Justice (2003) *Redeeming the Time: all God's people must challenge racism*, London: Churches Together in Britain and Ireland*

Cumbria Education Service (2004) *Ally Comes to Cumbria*, Carlisle: CES*

Department for Education and Skills (2004) *Aiming High: understanding the needs of minority ethnic pupils in mainly white schools*, London: DfES

Dunmore, Helen (2001) *The Siege*, London: Viking

East Sussex County Council (2004) *One of Us*, Brighton: East Sussex Education and Libraries

Evans, Iolo Wyn (1984) Chemistry, in Alma Craft and Geoffrey Bardell, eds, *Curriculum Opportunities in a Multicultural Society*, London: Harper and Row

Ewart, Franzeska (1998) *Let the Shadows Speak: developing children's language through shadow puppetry*, Stoke on Trent: Trentham Books

Fasheh, Munir (1980) Mathematics, Culture, and Authority, International Congress on Mathematical Education, California: Berkeley

Fisher, H.A.L. (1936) *A History of Europe*, London: Edward Arnold

Frank, Otto and Mirjam Pressler, eds (1997) *The Diary of a Young Girl*, London: Viking

Friedman, Edie (2002) *Making a Difference: promoting race equality in secondary schools, youth groups and adult education*, London: Jewish Council for Racial Equality*

Friedman, Edie and Hazel Woolfson, Sheila Freedman and Shirley Murgraff (2003) *Let's Make a Difference: teaching antiracism in primary schools*, London: Jewish Council for Racial Equality*

Fuglesang, Andreas (1982) *About Understanding: ideas and understandings on cross-cultural communication*, Uppsala: Dag Hammarskjöld Foundation, 1982.

Fulghum, Robert (1990) *All I Really Need To Know I Learned In Kindergarten*, New York: Villard Books

Gurnah, Abdulrazak (1988) *Pilgrim's Way*, London: Jonathan Cape

Hare, David (1995) *Skylight*, London: Faber and Faber

Hemmings, Ray (1984) Mathematics, in Alma Craft and Geoffrey Bardell, eds, *Curriculum Opportunities in a Multicultural Society*, London: Harper and Row

Home Office (2004) *Strength in Diversity: towards a community cohesion and race equality strategy*, London: Home Office

Hutchinson, Marcia, ed (2000) *The Journey*, Huddersfield: Primary Colours*

Imran, Muhammad and Elaine Miskell (2003) *Citizenship and Muslim Perspectives: teachers sharing ideas*, Birmingham: Tide Centre* and London: Islamic Relief*

Inter Faith Network (2004) *Connect: different faiths, shared values*, London: Inter Faith Network*

Ishiguro, Kazuo (1989) *The Remains of the Day*, London: Faber and Faber

Jaggi, Maya (1999) From Writing Back to Rewriting Britain, in Arts Council of England, *Whose Heritage? – the impact of cultural diversity on Britain's living heritage*, London: Arts Council

James, C L R (1963) *Beyond a Boundary: cricket and West Indian self-determination*, London and New York: Routledge

Jeyasingh, Shobana (1997) Interview, *British Studies Now* no. 9, April, London: British Council

Jowell, Tessa (2004) *Government and the value of culture: a personal view,* London: Department for Culture, Media and the Arts

Kearney, Chris (2004) *The Monkey's Mask: identity, memory, narrative and voice,* Stoke on Trent: Trentham Books

Klein, Gillian and Michael Marland, eds (2003) *A Vision for Today: John Eggleston's writings on education,* Stoke on Trent: Trentham

Koestler, Arthur (1964) *The Act of Creation,* London: Penguin Arkana

Kundnani, Arun (2004) In Memory of Blair Peach: an analysis of the changing face of racism, *Race Equality Teaching,* vol 22 no 3, summer

Levi, Primo (1975) *The Periodic Table,* reissued by Penguin Modern Classics, 2000

Lodge, David (2001) *Thinks,* London: Secker and Warburg

Lunan, Maggie and Susan McIntosh (2002) *Your Place or Mine? – exploring land issues in Scotland and South Africa,* Edinburgh: Scottish Development Education Centre*

MacCarthy, Fiona (1982) *William Morris: a life for our time,* London: Faber and Faber

Maitland, Sara (1993) *Home Truths,* London: Chatto and Windus

Mandela, Nelson (2002) *Madiba Magic,* Cape Town: Tafelberg, 2002.

National Union of Teachers (1993, revised 2001) *Anti-Racist Curriculum Guidelines,* London: NUT

Newton, Eric (1960) *The Arts of Man,* London: Thames and Hudson

O'Farrell, John (2001) *Global Village Idiot,* London: Doubleday

Patten, Chris (2003) Shaping Good Fortune, in Voluntary Service Overseas, ed, *Cultural Breakthrough: the defining moments,* VSO*

Phillips, Caryl (2001) *A New World Order: selected essays,* London: Secker and Warburg

Phillips, Caryl (2000) *The Atlantic Sound,* London: Vintage

Perera, Shyama (2004) One Small Step, in Rehana Ahmed, ed, *Walking a Tightrope: new writing from Asian Britain,* London: Young Picador

Qualifications and Curriculum Authority (2003) *Respect for All,* website at www.qca.org

Richardson, Robin and Berenice Miles (2003) *Equality Stories: recognition, respect and raising achievement,* Stoke on Trent: Trentham Books

Runnymede Trust (1993) *Equality Assurance in Schools: quality, identity and society,* Stoke on Trent: Trentham Books

Runnymede Trust (2003) *Complementing Teachers: a practical guide to promoting race equality in schools,* Granada Learning

Said, Edward (1993) *Culture and Imperialism,* London: Chatto and Windus

Sawney, Nitin (2003) Trust and Betrayal, in Voluntary Service Overseas, ed, *Cultural Breakthrough: defining moments,* VSO*

School Development Support Agency (2004) *Curriculum Reflecting Experiences of African Caribbean and Muslim Pupils,* Leicester: SDSA for the Department of Education and Skills*

Searle, Chris (1985) All Our Words, *World Studies Journal* vol 5 no 3

Seth, Vikram (1999) *Silent Music,* London: Phoenix House

Simawe, Saadi (2003) *Iraqi Poetry Today,* Exeter: Short Run Press

Sibbit, Rae (1997) *The Perpetrators of Racial Harassment and Racial Violence,* London: Home Office

Smith, David (2003) *If the World Were a Village,* London: A and C Black

Syal, Meera (2003) Last Laugh, in Voluntary Service Overseas, ed, *Cultural Breakthrough: defining moments,* VSO*

Team Video (2004) *Celebrating Diversity: inclusion in practice from age 3-7 years,* London: Team Video*

Thompson, Flora (1939) *Lark Rise to Candleford,* Oxford University Press, re-ssued by Penguin Books, 1973

Tide Centre (2001) *Globalisation – what's it all about?,* Birmingham: Tide

Voluntary Service Overseas (2003) *Cultural Breakthrough: defining moments,* London: VSO*

Walker, Alice (1982) *The Color Purple,* New York: Pocket Books

Ward, Barbara (1976) *The Home of Man,* London: Penguin Books

Warner, Marina (1994) *Managing Monsters,* London: Viking

Williams, Rowan (1999) *On Christian Theology,* Oxford: Blackwell

Williams, Rowan (2002) *Writing in the Dust,* London: Hodder and Stoughton

Wood, Angela (1984) Religious Education, in Alma Craft and Geoffrey Bardell, eds, *Curriculum Opportunities in a Multicultural Society,* London: Harper and Row

Wren, Brian (1977) *Education for Justice,* London: SCM Press

Zephaniah, Benjamin (2001) *We Are Britain,* London: Frances Lincoln

Addresses of organisations cited

Anne Frank Trust, Star House, 104-108 Grafton Road, London NW5 4BA (020 7284 5858) www.annefrank.org.uk

Birmingham Advisory Support Service, Martineau Centre, Balden Road, Harborne, Birmingham B32 2EH.

Churches Together in Britain and Ireland, Publications Department, 4 John Wesley Road, Peterborough PE4 6ZP (01733 325002) www.ctbi.org.uk/ccrj/welcome.htm

Cumbria Education Service, 5 Portland Square, Carlisle CA1 1PU

Tide Centre, G04 Millennium Point, Curzon Street, Birmingham B4 7XG (0121 202 3290) www.tidec.org

Inter Faith Network for the United Kingdom, 8A Lower Grosvenor Place, London SW1W 0EN (020 7931 7766) www.interfaith.org.uk

Insted Consultancy, 14 High Street, Wembley, Middlesex HA9 8DD (020 8900 1720) www.insted.co.uk

Intermediate Technology Group, Bourton Hall, Bourton-on-Dunsmore, Rugby CV23 9QZ (01926 634400) www.itdg.org

Islamic Relief, Unit 40 Uplands Business Park, Blackhorse Lane, London E17 5QJ

Jewish Council for Racial Equality, 35 Seymour Place, London W1H 6AU (020 8455 0896) www.jcore.org.uk

Primary Colours, PO Box 436, Huddersfield HD2 1FT

School Development Support Agency, Room 114, Town Hall, Leicester LE1 9BG (0116 299 5942)

Scottish Development Education Centre, The Courtyard Rooms, Simon Laurie House, Holyrood Campus, Edinburgh EH9 8AQ (0131 557 6087) www.scotdec.org.uk

Soul of Europe, The Coach House, Church Street, Crediton, Devon EX17 2AQ (01363 775100) www.soulofeurope.org

Team Video, Canalot, 222 Kensal Road, London W10 5BN (020 8960 5536), www.team-video.co.uk

Voluntary Service Overseas, 317 Putney Bridge Road, London SW15 2PN (020 8780 7200) www.vso.org.uk